Kelly,

Love You

Stefan!

XO,

BDH

BETH LINDSAY CHAPMAN     CANDICE COPPOLA     CARLA TEN EYCK

# THE WHITE DRESS
## *Destinations*

### THE DEFINITIVE GUIDE TO
### PLANNING THE *new* DESTINATION WEDDING

Schiffer
Publishing Ltd

4880 Lower Valley Road • Atglen, PA 19310

Library of Congress Control Number: 2017949345

Layout by Justin Watkinson
Cover by Danielle D. Farmer
Photography by Carla Ten Eyck
Type set in Neutra Text/MissLeGatees

ISBN: 978-0-7643-5303-1
Printed in China

Published by Schiffer Publishing, Ltd.
4880 Lower Valley Road
Atglen, PA 19310
Phone: (610) 593-1777; Fax: (610) 593-2002
E-mail: Info@schifferbooks.com

For our complete selection of fine books on this and related subjects,
please visit our website at **www.schifferbooks.com**. You may also write for a free catalog.

Schiffer Publishing's titles are available at special discounts for bulk purchases for sales promotions or premiums. Special editions, including personalized covers, corporate imprints, and excerpts, can be created in large quantities for special needs. For more information, contact the publisher.

We are always looking for people to write books on new and related subjects.
If you have an idea for a book, please contact us at **proposals@schifferbooks.com**.

Other Schiffer Books by the Authors:

THE WHITE DRESS IN COLOR: *Wedding Inspirations for the Modern Bride,*
978-0-7643-4567-8, $45.00

Other Schiffer Books on Related Subjects:

THE PAINTER'S WEDDING: *Inspired Celebrations with an Artistic Edge,*
by Kristy Rice, 978-0-7643-5442-7, $34.99

## CANDICE

To my husband, "my person," thank you for always stealing a kiss while I'm washing the dishes, encouraging me to work hard, being the voice of reason in our lives, making me laugh every day, and loving me unconditionally. I love you—let's make magic! To Beth and Carla, our careers have been a journey, woven together throughout these past nine years. I'm grateful for every laugh, tear, hug, and bottle of wine we've shared. I'd like to dedicate this book to my friend and creative partner-in-crime, Nichole Michel.

## CARLA

I am so thankful to my Jack Bibbs and Georgie Picklepuss for their generous hearts, and grateful that I am able to show them what a happy, inspired, and fulfilled momma is! I want to thank my mom and dad for always supporting me and my dream of pursuing a life filled with photography, art, and light. To my coauthors and creative partners-in-crime, Beth and Candice, for pushing through and making this beautiful book happen. To my girl Chloe for her styling talent, support, and friendship.

## BETH

To my family, especially my husband Mark, for always believing in me and encouraging me to follow my dreams. To my beautiful children, Lindsay and Mark, you inspire me to be a better person every day. To my talented team at The White Dress by the Shore, thank you for your support and holding down the fort while I pursue my love of styling. To Nichole, thank you for lending your creative talents to this project and for being a good friend. To my coauthors and dear friends, Candice and Carla, I could not think of two people that I would rather be on this journey with! And finally, to God, my biggest supporter, without your love and grace, nothing is possible.

CONTENTS

richard
gulkin

frederick
diehl

claire
reddington

charles
darbonne

stephanie
suskind

emma
holmes

# Introduction

Destination dreams. Over the past decade, the number of couples dreaming of (and planning) a romantic destination wedding has skyrocketed. And never before has a destination wedding been more within reach. As the world gets smaller, far-flung destinations once thought impractical and off-limits are now a magnificent reality for wedding couples and their guests. In this gorgeous new book from industry powerhouses Beth Chapman, Candice Coppola, and Carla Ten Eyck, the dreams of destinations near and far, from Barbados to Paris, are brought to life in an innovative way.

The beauty of a destination wedding is that couples and their guests are transported far from the day-to-day realities of life, and their time together is magnified in a way that creates meaningful and lifelong connections. What better way to officially begin life together than surrounded by those nearest and dearest, and to bond in a way that simply cannot happen with a hometown wedding that lasts only a few hours and might bring distractions and obligations.

Like any wonderful wedding, this book is a true collaboration. Bringing their years of experience working with couples from around the world, this dynamic dream team partnered with the best of the best to create stunning visual inspiration and balance it with practical advice to make what could be an overwhelming process just what it should be: exciting, personal, and above all, fun!

Through their keen design and style sense, Beth, Candice, and Carla have captured the romance and magic of a destination wedding. Readers are transported to different parts of the world to get a sense of just how unique a destination wedding can be.

*Rebecca Grinnals*
*&*
*Kathryn Arce*

**Celebration**, Florida, February 2017
Engaging Concepts + producers of Engage!
The Luxury Wedding Business Summit

"*I haven't been everywhere,* BUT IT'S ON MY LIST."

—Susan Sontag

# Planning a Bespoke
## DESTINATION
## WEDDING
### Candice Coppola

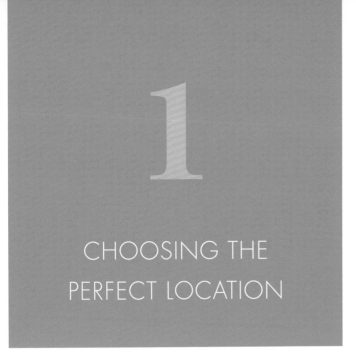

# 1

## CHOOSING THE PERFECT LOCATION

Planning a destination wedding, like marriage, is an adventure! I'm glad you and your betrothed have decided to break with tradition by choosing to travel to a magnificent place to exchange your vows. A destination wedding is a one-of-a-kind experience for your guests and a memory you will cherish together. Destination weddings are typically weekend-long affairs with opportunities for the attendees to get to know one another and form friendships. It can be a little like summer camp, but for adults! And who doesn't love summer camp?

There are so many beautiful places to get married, which makes it difficult to decide on a location. Before you become overwhelmed, sit down with your partner and answer some of the following questions:

- What are our top priorities for a destination wedding? An adventurous location? Good food? Unique atmosphere? Cultural experience? Luxury resort? A place our guests have never visited? A location significant to us?
- How much are we willing to spend on our wedding?
- How many guests do we want to invite?
- Do we want our wedding to be small and intimate or large and over-the-top?
- Where do we **not** want to have a destination wedding?

Your answers to these questions will help guide you to the right destination on the map.

Most couples choose a location that has some special meaning; perhaps you were engaged during a trip to Paris, or you have fond memories of family vacations on the coast of Maine. Looking at places you've been and return to, time and time again, is a great place to start. Also, knowing what style of wedding you want will guide you in the right direction. A beach wedding on the shores of the Caribbean sounds like a magical evening, or perhaps you want to have a rustic, luxurious winter wedding in Aspen. It's crucial to understand what style

**Same-sex weddings.** As you begin to research wedding locations, keep in mind that not all countries are same-sex friendly. Some welcoming countries are: United States, Argentina, Canada, Belgium, Brazil, France, Denmark, New Zealand, The Netherlands, Iceland, Portugal, Spain, Sweden, and Norway.

**Local accommodations.** If your wedding venue is not a hotel or resort, make sure adequate accommodations are available. Ask nearby hotels about pricing and availability. A good rule of thumb is to provide two options to your guests at varying price points: one on the higher-end and one in a moderate price range. You might be able to achieve this at only one hotel by offering two different room types (ocean view or garden view). Hotels will almost always give you a group rate when you inquire about a room block. A room block is a specified number of rooms blocked off for the dates you've indicated, under your group name, so guests can make discounted reservations. Securing a room block not only saves your guests money, but it is also an easy way for you to track where your guests are staying so you can provide adequate transportation and deliver welcome bags.

of wedding appeals to the both of you as you research locations. Not all destination weddings have to be in a tropical location (although most guests love jetting away for a weekend in Barbados!). Here are some other ideas for a memorable location:

- A rustic wedding at a luxurious ranch in Montana
- A vineyard-style affair in the Russian River Valley
- An intimate elopement in historic Vancouver, British Columbia
- A modern affair nestled along the white coast of Santorini
- An artsy fete in the hills of Montmartre
- A wedding with southern charm and hospitality in Charleston

Guests will thank you for choosing a location that is easily accessible. Unless you will be providing airfare and transportation, do your best to select a location with a direct flight from your local airport. Research airfare during the times of year you are looking to get married to understand how much your guests will pay for their flights. Some destinations are cheaper toward the beginning or end of their tourist seasons, and locations are almost always less expensive in their off season.

It is important to know what is happening in your destination during the time you plan to be there. Do some research on the local climate—you want to avoid a country's rainy season. Find out if any large events, such as festivals, are taking place just before, during, or after your wedding. This could leave you with a shortage of accommodations, flights, and vendors. Many European cities virtually shut down during July and August, as those who live there go on holiday.

**Duties and taxes.** For weddings outside your country of residence, you may need to pay duties and taxes for goods you import. This can be anything you ship by air or sea and can include items such as welcome bags, linens, and even flowers. Every country has its own percentage of duties and taxes levied against goods, and the process is often confusing. A wedding planner in the region can help you hire a customs broker who will manage your cargo, pay duties on your behalf, and also source items locally so you don't have to find extra room in your budget for taxes. Your best bet is to pack as much as you can in your suitcases and recruit kind friends and family to help with transport. Still, be prepared to pay duties on items if they're found while going through customs at the airport.

Once you've narrowed your top destinations to three or four, begin investigating locations for your ceremony and reception. Couples often choose a hotel or resort as home base. If you are a frequent guest at a resort such as Four Seasons, ask them about their wedding packages. If you prefer a smaller, more intimate location, tourist destinations have many boutique hotels at a variety of price points. A hotel or resort provides many conveniences:

- You and your guests can stay on site, which eliminates the need for transportation to and from wedding-day activities.
- They have on-site wedding planners who can guide you through the process of hiring vendors and obtaining your marriage license.
- They have many amenities on-site, such as spa services, catering, staffing, and rentals.

If a hotel is not the right fit, other popular options are unique restaurants, historic sites, gardens, beaches, parks, and villas. These options allow you to customize your wedding. Imagine getting married in a fifteenth-century estate in Tuscany or a redwood forest in Northern California. The possibilities are endless.

If all this research is overwhelming, enlist the help of a wedding planner. Wedding planners have exclusive access to locations you may not stumble upon yourself. They can be hired to do all the venue research and provide you with a list of options that meet your criteria. A wedding planner may also be necessary if you are booking a villa or private home, as the level of logistics will likely require an expert.

Keep in mind that not all destinations have good access to specialty décor and vendors. The flowers and rentals you can find with ease in New York City will most likely not be available on the picturesque island of St. Lucia, unless you are willing to spend the money to import it. No doubt you have thumbed through the glossy pages of a bridal magazine or two since getting engaged. If you are dreaming of using some of the distinct décor you've seen in magazines or on wedding blogs, be sure those items are available. Hosting your wedding near a large city or in a prominent wedding destination will yield a variety of décor options, from specialty tents to glittering chandeliers and the perfect gold charger plate. In remote destinations, such as smaller island nations, you are not likely to find the same robust inventory.

I also encourage you to make at least one trip to your destination before signing any contracts, especially if you've never been there. A visit can also help you avoid making costly mistakes by vetting your vendors in person and seeing the location where your wedding will be held. Make a long weekend out of it and invite family or close friends to help you make decisions. If you have invested in a wedding planner at your destination, this is a great opportunity to work together face to face.

Ultimately, the location is the biggest "character" in your wedding style, so choose wisely! Just like you knew your partner was the one, you will know when you find the right destination. It will embody all the criteria you determined was important, and will organically have the look and feel of the wedding you want.

# 2

## BUDGETING

The financial aspect of a wedding is often the most stressful. Know that you will experience sticker shock. For this reason, it's important to thoroughly research your wedding destination to make sure it coincides with what you can afford.

When I sit down with clients, one of the first things I need to know is how much they want to spend. Most couples have no idea what amount is reasonable. This is one of the benefits of having an experienced wedding planner; it is our job to know what things cost based on our years of research.

Start by asking each other: what number do we not want to go over? What is our financial comfort zone and what number would set us over the edge? You'll need to have frank discussions about money throughout your marriage, so now is a good time to begin.

If someone is helping you pay for the wedding, ask them what they are willing to contribute. Couples always find this conversation difficult, so if you are feeling squeamish about asking your parents how big the check will be, know that you are not alone! However, understanding what everyone is contributing will help you develop a realistic budget.

Many wedding-industry guides assign certain percentages of costs to services. This approach can help you anticipate what you'll spend, but these are not rules. No one says you have to spend ten percent on your wedding photographer or fifteen percent on your wedding rings. Your wedding is as unique as the both of you, and you should not subscribe to prescribed spending rules.

In preparing your budget, consider what events you would like to host:

WELCOME PARTY: This event usually occurs a few days before the wedding, on the day in which most guests arrive. It can be an informal gathering for cocktails at a scenic location or dinner on a secluded beach at sunset. The welcome party is a great way for your guests to get to know one another.

REHEARSAL DINNER: Your rehearsal dinner usually takes place the night before the wedding and should have an entirely different feel than your wedding day. I encourage you to invite all your guests, but it is also acceptable to invite only immediate family members and your bridal party. If you choose not to invite all your guests, this gives them a free evening to explore and dine at a restaurant of their choice.

**More isn't always merrier.** The easiest way to trim your costs is to invite fewer guests. You will not only save on food and beverages, but also rentals, transportation, décor, staffing, floral design, gifts, and many other items. Each guest will not only need a meal and a stiff drink, but also a seat at the table (and on the bus!), a plate, knife, fork, favor, and invitation.

**POST-WEDDING BRUNCH:** I love the post-wedding brunch because it's a great way to spend time with your guests before everyone heads home. Keep it informal and start a little later in the morning so guests can sleep in. Your guests will thank you for feeding them before their ride to the airport. Consider offering a bloody Mary bar or mimosas to take the edge off that post-wedding hangover! In lieu of a brunch, put together breakfast to-go kits that the hotel can give your guests when they check out.

**OTHER ACTIVITIES:** There are all sorts of activities to which you may want to treat your guests: a catamaran cruise, an island tour with drinks and lunch, a day of skiing at a nearby resort, or a trip to a local vineyard for a wine tasting. The point is to explore and have fun together. Your guests never expect paid-for activities, so don't feel obligated if you are trying to conserve costs—but they are appreciated!

Once you've determined the additional events and activities you'll host, it's time to put together your wedding budget. Based on the following list of categorized items, prioritize what is most important, with one being the most important and five being the least important. I've grouped different categories of items as they relate to some of the largest expenses for your wedding day/weekend. Prioritizing them will give you a clearer picture of where to invest funds and where you can scale back. You and your partner may find that your answers are very similar or very different.

**AMBIANCE AND DESIGN:** From custom linens to sumptuous flowers, the glow of candlelight, and tents swathed in fabric, your wedding design is the environment your guests will experience on the big day. Is décor important to you? Do you want to transport your guests not only to another country, but to a designed party environment they've never seen before? Items included in this category are flowers, paper, rentals, lighting, and any décor details you invest in to personalize your wedding day.

**ENTERTAINMENT:** Music and special performances make up this category. Do you want to hire a live band for the reception? Are you headed somewhere exotic and want to hire local dancers to perform during your rehearsal dinner?

**FOOD AND BEVERAGES:** This line item is typically the largest expense and includes everything your guests will eat and drink on your wedding day or throughout the weekend. Do you want to provide them with a unique culinary experience?

GUEST EXPERIENCE: This includes elements that delight your guests or aid in their comfort, including accommodations, transportation, favors and gifts, additional events, and the wedding planner and designer who will put all of those pieces together. Is your guests' comfort important? Do you want them to feel like every part of their experience has been designed just for them?

PHOTOGRAPHY AND VIDEOGRAPHY: Do you dream about what your wedding photographs will look like? Is having a specific wedding photographer important? Do you want a cinematic video to share with friends and family who couldn't attend? Besides your marriage license and the vows you exchanged, all you have left from your wedding day are the photographs and cinematography.

**You can ask, but don't expect discounts**. It is okay to ask a vendor if they would be willing to decrease their price or remove a service to meet your budget. However, don't expect businesses to give you discounts or lower their pricing significantly. It isn't that they don't want your business, but they may not be able to lower their cost without taking a loss. Almost all wedding vendors are small businesses that have developed unique skills and services—and those skills come at a cost. Another approach is to ask a company if they can add any extra value at the same price; this can be an added service, an extra hour, an assistant on wedding day, or more product.

It is a good idea to create a unique budget for each event you are hosting. Divide your wedding budget into the following line items as they relate to you:

Accommodations

Beauty

Cake and confections

Décor

Entertainment

Fashion, including gowns,
   accessories, and tuxes/suits

Favors and gift bags

Floral design

Food and beverage

Gratuity

Invitations and stationery

Miscellaneous

Officiant

Photographer

Rentals and equipment

Staffing

Transportation and travel

Videographer

Wedding planner
   and/or designer

Wedding site fees

It's okay if you can't afford every idea you have. Treating your guests to a unique and memorable experience is what is important, so invest in the areas that matter most to you. Above all, stay within your means. Don't take out credit cards or loans to pay for one day in your life; be responsible and be honest about what you can afford.

**Gratuity is a gift**. Gratuity is a gift for exemplary service. It is for those who go above and beyond the job you've hired them for, exceeding your expectations. Gratuity is never expected, but always appreciated. Make sure you understand the areas where gratuity has already been included—commonly your catering team, bartending staff, and hotel staff. You can choose to tip any vendor or business, and it is perfectly acceptable to tip the business owner if they are the individual working your wedding. Common professionals to tip are: musicians, wait staff, delivery drivers, wedding planners, photographers, videographers, entertainers, DJs, bus and limo drivers, bridal dresser, hair and makeup artists, and anyone else who you have hired. The amount of your tips is up to you— it is a gift, after all.

# 3

# IMPLEMENTING YOUR DESTINATION WEDDING STYLE

Couples seem to love the creative aspect of destination wedding planning the most! It is a chance to embrace the colors, textures, patterns, fabrics, food, and signature cocktails you love—elements that cater to all five senses. Sometimes, however, finding your wedding style can feel overwhelming given the sheer number of available options. That's why I want you to take a breath, stop Googling "rustic modern whimsical wedding," and start with the biggest character and design element you have: your location.

Earlier, I asked you to choose a location that complements the wedding style you envision. That's because the location is the largest source of inspiration. It can come from almost anywhere: wallpaper in a hotel lobby, a beautiful garden where the ceremony will be held, a signature dish at a restaurant, or the scenic views surrounding the reception venue. There is a reason why you and your partner fell in love with a specific hotel, historical site, or restaurant—so use it as the first source of inspiration.

What colors do you see? Are there any patterns in art, furniture, or fixtures? If you had to describe the style of your wedding location, what adjectives would you use? Is it rustic, modern, classic, preppy, or bohemian? Maybe it is a quirky mixture of a few, perfectly balanced elements and unique unto itself (just like you). What is the vibe, the essence, the soul of the location or city? Your answers will help tremendously in mixing the style of your location with your personal style.

By embracing the uniqueness of your surroundings, you also save money on décor and rentals. By contrast, when you choose a location that needs a heavy transformation, you spend a lot of money to make the space more **you**. Work with what you've got and enhance it as you see fit.

Later in this book you'll see examples of how we took styling cues from the destination. Pay attention to how we used local character to create a wedding that echoes its setting.

The second source of inspiration comes from your personal style—how you decorate your home, the clothing you wear, and what you gravitate to stylistically. A wedding style or theme is best represented when it portrays you and what you like. I'm always flattered when a guest approaches me at a wedding I've designed and says, "Wow—this is so beautiful, and so them!" That means I did a good job listening to what the couple likes. I have a hunch that you've chosen a location that is already indicative of your personal style, so you are one step ahead in implementing your weddings design.

Consider the following elements as bespoke, design-worthy components of the wedding day or weekend. These are places where you can infuse a mixture of the organic regional style and your own style to create a unique experience for your guests. Pick and choose what to customize based on your priorities and what you've budgeted for.

## FOOD

The menu you craft is one of the most important, memorable, and expensive elements of your wedding. The dishes you serve are a great place to feature your style and your destination. Ask your caterer what types of food the location is known for. Whether you are getting married in the United States or abroad, every region has its signature dishes. For example, if you are getting married in Northern California, incorporating local cheeses and wine is a great nod to your destination. If your nuptials are in the Caribbean, locally fished seafood, exotic fruits, and West Indian dishes like curry make a great menu. If you are having a rustic, romantic wedding in the green hills of Tuscany, consider dining on a variety of freshly baked breads, locally raised poultry, handcrafted pasta, seasonal vegetables, and a signature dessert. Play up regionally sourced food while mixing in some of your favorite dishes to create a unique culinary experience.

Cocktail hour is an opportunity to add variety by including both local fare and personal favorites. Consider offering two to three passed hors d'oeuvres that represent the region, while also serving two to three familiar options. You'll want diverse gastronomic options that will please a gluten-free guest, a vegetarian guest, bacon-lovers, and those allergic to shellfish. Presentation can personalize the look and feel of your wedding, too. Collaborate with your caterer on the style of trays used to serve hors d'oeuvres. Planning a wedding with a modern look? Consider using sleek white resin trays. Want pops of color? Add custom-made paper liners in a bold color with a design element or pattern from your invitations.

For this food pairing, our caterer designed trays that hold a tasty quesadilla on a modern square plate alongside a tequila cocktail in miniature Don Julio bottles.

The signature cocktail, a traditional gin martini with a twist, reflects the vibe of the grooms and the wedding design.

# BEVERAGES

Arguably every guest's favorite part of a wedding is the cocktails, mocktails, and refreshingly delicious drinks. Have fun creating a unique drink menu for your wedding day, including local alcohol and other beverages in the bar fare. Designing some fun signature cocktails for your wedding is a great way to pull in your style (and also a good excuse to do a lot of pre-wedding taste testing!). Here in Barbados, a rum punch is the signature cocktail. If you are getting married in New Orleans, how about a spin on the famous Hurricane? Tequila goes without saying in Mexico; Ireland is known for its whiskey, and in Kentucky the Mint Julep is a nod to the Derby. The point is to have fun and play with an element that already exists. You can put a spin on any cocktail by switching up a few ingredients, changing how it is served, using a cool straw, adding a custom drink stirrer, or simply purchasing locally sourced spirits.

The bar area is another opportunity to highlight a style or theme. Skip the banquet table with linen and opt for a real bar and unique bar back. I was inspired by the chinoiserie pattern and boxwood for this photo shoot, so I incorporated those elements into the bar display. I took the bespoke design further with a custom chandelier in our recurring blue and white pattern, which hung above the faux boxwood bar. There were even fun decorative props among the glassware and spirits in the bar back. Bar carts are trendy and easy to style, and can serve as a signature drink station. In subsequent chapters, you'll see some of our bar cart ideas.

# PAPER

Your wedding paper is probably the easiest element to personalize. There are so many options to choose from and the best way to get started is to look through books, magazines, blogs, and Pinterest to see what jumps out at you. The design of your invitation will set the tone for the rest of your paper, including ceremony programs, escort cards, menus, place cards, and signage.

Nautical touches carry through to the paper story, from the gold glitter anchor on the front of the invitation, to the classic nautical stripe. The language echoes the theme, inviting guests to share in "the sun, the sea, and the memories."

Together with their families
**Paige Caldwell**
✳ ✳ AND ✳ ✳
*Noah Reynolds*
look forward to sharing with you
the sun, the sea and the memories
of their wedding celebration

*four in the afternoon*
JUNE 23 — TWO THOUSAND THIRTEEN
Saint Mary's Church
STONINGTON, CONNECTICUT

*Dinner, dancing and eternity to follow*

com

When designing your paper, have fun with the use of typography, color, patterns, and motifs (or not, if clean design is your thing). If there is a guiding element of your wedding design, bring it into your invitations! I've worked with couples who used a pattern from their mother's favorite china; another couple was inspired by Kate Spade and chose a feminine invitation with bold pops of color, gold confetti, and a popped champagne motif.

Several online retailers have a robust selection of invitations at varying price points. This outlet is usually a great option if you don't mind minimal personalization and are looking for reasonably priced designed paper.

If you want custom designed invitations, which are more expensive, start with stationers and paper designers in your area. However, don't feel limited to brick and mortar stores in your town or city; you can work with a paper artist whose work you love from anywhere in the world! Long gone are the days of flipping through the enormous invitation book and selecting a prefabricated design. When working with a custom designer, you can literally do anything your heart desires.

Have fun bringing in touches from your invitation into the entire paper suite of your wedding. Carry through the color and design elements with your menu cards, escort cards, place cards, table numbers, ceremony programs, bar signs, and any other fabulous paper details you dream up, including your guests' out-of-town bags!

# GIFTS & OUT-OF-TOWN BAGS

An out-of-town welcome bag is the perfect way to welcome guests as they arrive at their hotel, villa, or condo after a day of traveling. In terms of design, keep your wedding's color palette, location, and style in mind when curating items for the bags. If you don't want to take on this task, there are some fabulous companies that specialize in wedding guest gifts. If you've hired a wedding planner, he or she can help you put together an amazing welcome gift within your budget.

This out-of-town bag complements the black-and-white wedding colors. Its contents ease the trip home: silver happy plugs, miniature Dominos set, comfy blanket, eye mask, bottle of water, and "The Carry-on Cocktail Kit" with two bottles of Tanqueray for one last gin and tonic.

I recommend putting together useful items guests might need during their stay. You can base the contents on a theme: local goodies, items to make their travel more enjoyable, or even a few of your favorite things. In our inspirational chapters you'll find some great ideas for out-of-town bags that were based on the design of each photo shoot.

Personalization has become a huge trend. If you have the budget to personalize items, have fun creating unique gifts. For example, if you are getting married in a tropical location, design a beach bag and fill it with custom-labeled water bottles, a uniquely designed plastic tumbler with nips and directions for making a cocktail, a beach towel in your wedding's color story, and local savory and sweet snacks. If you are on a tight budget, stick with quality over quantity and include items for them to snack on. Whether you've allocated a lot or a little to the welcome bag budget, remember to purchase items your guests will appreciate.

This is also the place to include a weekend itinerary and a welcome note, thanking your guests for making the journey. No matter which direction you go for this special detail, guests will love your thoughtfulness.

## CAKE & CONFECTIONS

Every guest anticipates dessert, so why not make the display fun? These days, most couples have a dessert station rather than a plated dessert so that guests can nibble at their leisure. It's also a great place to pull in your style.

If you are getting married in Paris, serve miniature macaroons, tarte tatin, crêpes, eclair au chocolate, madeleines, and a croquembouche in place of a traditional wedding cake. Use cake stands and beautiful trays, and embellish the display with calligraphy that details the name of each dessert. Is Mexico your destination? Then serve individual flans, Mexican chocolate, lime margarita bars, and warm churros.

If you don't want to ditch the wedding cake, embrace the tradition and base its design on an element of your wedding. Popular sources of inspiration are: wedding fashion, flowers used in your décor, a pattern or motif from your invitation, or simply the wedding colors. You can also customize the flavor to the region—remember, you want a cake that not only looks beautiful, but tastes even better! Ask your baker to make colorful layers that coordinate with the wedding's color palette. You'll find inspiration for beautiful cakes and confections in subsequent chapters.

## FLOWERS

Flowers are one of my favorite elements of wedding design, and in my wildest wedding dreams, I see flowers everywhere: dripping from a ceremony canopy, overflowing from a candlelit tablescape, adorning every place setting's napkin and

guest chair, and even hanging from the ceiling. If you love flowers, it's important that you work with a floral designer who understands your vision. Save images of floral arrangements, bouquets, and other flower details that speak to you. If you're having a rustic wedding, look for flowers arranged in a loose and organic way. If modern and streamlined is your style, find arrangements that have clean lines and unique containers. If you want something avant-garde, work with your floral designer to dream up a design that will have your guests talking. Your florist should be able to interpret your style once you show examples of what you like.

Consider using flowers in your ceremony, which includes bouquets, boutonnières, and any flowers a guest of honor will wear or carry. Your ceremony setting will normally have some floral decoration, be it the chuppah, flowers hung from a large oak tree that is the focal point for your ceremony, or large urns filled with blooms at the alter. You can add swags of greenery to the chairs, clutches of flowers to your church pews, and petals scattered down the aisle. The ceremony is the reason everyone is there, so the setting should look special and reflect you.

For the reception area, consider centerpieces in containers or garlands hanging down the edges of the table, or a single bloom or sprig of rosemary at every place setting. Dress your cocktail tables with terrariums of succulents, include bud vases of ranunculus on the bar, or design flower chandeliers for your tent. The possibilities are endless! The best advice I can offer is to have fun with flowers if they are a priority budget item.

A common misconception is that you have to have a lot of flowers to make a big impact. I'm here to tell you that is not true! Your bridesmaids don't have to carry an overflowing bouquet of luscious blooms—a beautiful, unique single flower can also make a state-ment. Nor do you have to carry a traditional round bouquet. Consider an architectural bouquet that hangs down like the one pictured. Bouquets don't have to be floral, either; they can be composed of greenery, garlands, leaves, or even fabric if that's more your aesthetic. Ultimately, flowers or their substitute should enhance the overall design by adding texture, color, and style.

Flowers, including greenery, can be expensive, as is a florist's design time. Set a budget early on and work with your wedding planner to find a florist who can comply with your spending plan. Your wedding planner can also tell you if your budget is feasible based on the quantity of flowers you envision and your design ideas.

The easiest way to spend money on flowers is to choose expensive blooms that are out of season. Conversely, you'll maximize your floral budget by not insisting on a specific flower (I *have* to have peonies!). Rather, request a style of arrangement and let the florist determine which variety of flowers would best achieve that style. That way, you open yourself up to choices that are more within your budget. I also like to find places to reuse flowers throughout the day. Bring those ceremony urns to your reception to dress up a fireplace, or reuse the flowers on your pews as door wreaths. As you work with a florist, think about ways to repurpose ceremony décor at the reception.

If you are heading to a tropical environment, remember that not all flowers thrive in high heat and humidity. Your floral designer can direct you to blooms that are appropriate to the climate.

You can, of course, avoid flowers altogether and stick with natural greens and warm candlelight. A long dining table with greenery and clusters of colorful Moroccan lanterns would look gorgeous at a sunset beach reception.

## LINENS & FABRICS

As a designer, I use linens and fabrics to reinforce the ambiance I want to convey. They are the perfect way to bring in a splash of color that can't be found in nature, like a brilliant turquoise or navy blue. Play around with patterns and texture, selecting table linens that work with the environment. If you are hosting a nautical-themed affair, consider a seersucker linen or even a polka dot. For a more rustic vibe, I love using linen or other natural fabrics in a muted hue. If you're getting married in the tropics, source a banana leaf-patterned linen for your cocktail tables! Napkins are another fun way to bring in a pattern or pop of color. Linens make a huge impact and may cost less than other design elements.

## CHARGERS, PLATES, FLATWARE & GLASSWARE

The accoutrements that make up a well-set dining table can be easily personalized with a little creativity and a good rental company. If you are getting married in a place where you can find unique charger plates, dinner plates, flatware, and glassware, consider pulling together a fully custom look. Each place setting at this table has a bronze charger plate, which was a color in our palette. We added gray patterned china with a silver rim, framed by bronze flatware inspired by the shape of a bumblebee. To finish it off, we found sleek, sexy glasses in a modern shape.

Usually, your reception venue or caterer will provide you with "house standard" plates, glasses, and flatware. You can choose to upgrade all these pieces to personalized items, or, if budget is a concern, add a charger plate or swap out the house flatware for something more your style. Even customizing one or two pieces can have a dramatic impact!

## LIGHTING

As any event designer will tell you, lighting is extremely important. It has the ability to instantly change ambiance and mood: flashing dance lights will put your guests in party mode, while candles and twinkle light invoke romance. It can also transform a space with a splash of color. Lighting allows you to downplay eyesores and enhance architectural features. It can make a vast space feel more intimate, or give small spaces a grander appeal. A good lighting scheme is the most effortless way to add big impact or create a mood.

In its simplest form, it can be candles on the table and tiki torches lining the beach. You can suspend glittering chandeliers above your tables, hang lighted crystals from trees, and use colored uplighting to amplify mood. Lighting also serves a practical purpose by brightening dark areas where guests need to see.

## FURNITURE

Chic modern lounges, rustic outdoor benches, and mismatched vintage furniture have all become trends in bespoke wedding design. Lounges give your guests a place to relax during cocktail hour and somewhere to sit and converse during the dance party. Do you have a love affair with midcentury modern furniture? Bring in Mad Men-esque chairs, couches, tables, and lamps to create a unique environment for your guests to enjoy.

Consider using antique church pews rather than the white wooden folding chairs for ceremony seating. Rectangular wooden tables can be dressed down for a rustic wedding, or can be given a glamorous look with overflowing flowers in crystal vases. Renting unique furniture for your wedding adds another level of personalization. Whatever furniture you choose, refer to your prioritized budget and stay true to your own style.

# 4

## HIRING DESTINATION WEDDING VENDORS

There are many talented people in the wedding industry, from photographers to floral designers and caterers. As you cultivate your creative team, keep your budget handy and let it guide you in finding the right vendors.

Consider several factors as you hire wedding services. First, look for businesses whose work you admire. Flip through their portfolio and read about their company's approach. Look for companies that have an intrinsic understanding of what you want for your wedding. Next, determine whose pricing aligns with what you are willing to spend. A friendly introductory email outlining the details of your wedding, with an inquiry about their pricing, is a good place to start. Remember the mention of sticker shock earlier? This is where you're going to experience it more than once! Not every business you contact will be within your price point. Keep in mind, too, that you are hiring them not only for their creativity, but also their experience and reputation.

I encourage you to hire a planner who is either local to your destination or familiar with it. It's a challenge to plan from afar given the differences in time, language, and culture. A wedding planner will guide you through the process and fiercely protect your priorities, helping you build a dream team of talented specialists. She or he will keep you on budget, on task, and recommend the right vendors. Your planner will have a database of professional vendors at varying price points, approaches, and aesthetics. Wedding planners manage all the logistical details and act as a liaison between you and your vendors, and on the big day they keep things running smoothly. Whether you are inviting twenty guests or 200, a wedding planner will help to alleviate the stress of your destination wedding. A wedding is an investment, and by hiring a wedding planner you are securing that investment against costly mistakes.

However, if you choose to go it alone, here are some tips for hiring vendors:

- Require vendors to send you a contract of services, which you can review prior to sending in any deposits. No matter how small the service, a contract is essential before money is exchanged.
- Ask for references who you can contact by phone or email. Any reputable business will be able to produce a list of references. Some businesses ask permission from their former clients to share contact information, so you may have to wait a few days.
- Ask if you can see work they've done at your wedding venue or similar to your style. A vendor's website might not have their latest work, so don't be afraid to ask if they have anything else to help you make your decision.
- If you have the means to travel, interview vendors face-to-face before hiring them, or use Skype or FaceTime.
- Hire as much local talent as you can. Your support of the local economy has a huge impact, and vendors will be grateful for the business.
- If you can't find a local specialist, look for a creative who specializes in destination weddings. In a later chapter, we'll discuss hiring a photographer whom you can bring to your destination. This is more costly, but worth it if you can't find the right fit on location. Remember that if you are flying someone into another country, they may need a work permit.

# 5

## GUEST ETIQUETTE, SAVE-THE-DATE CARDS, AND INVITATIONS

A common misconception is that by having a destination wedding you can have a smaller, more intimate affair because not all of your guests will be able to make the trip. That is a dangerous assumption! If you invite someone to your wedding, expect that they will RSVP with a resounding yes! Although the industry average of declines is roughly twenty percent (higher for destination weddings), be sure your wedding budget can sustain every person on your list.

Putting together a guest list can be challenging. Use whatever format works best for you: an Excel spreadsheet, online wedding planning software, or notebook where you can jot down names. Start with immediate family members and close friends. Tally up the numbers and decide whether you have room for more.

If you do, ask your parents who they would like to invite in addition to the names you've collected. You will especially want their input if they are chipping in financially. If you and your partner prefer a small guest list, let your parents know your target number so they can keep it in mind as they prepare their list. Don't be surprised if they send back to you a lengthy list of names, including many you do not even know! A gentle reminder of what you want will prompt them to reevaluate their list.

Knowing whom to invite can be tricky, especially taking into consideration family dynamics and others' expectations. My advice is to stick to your budget and select people who have loved and supported you in your life. Those two guiding principles should make this process easier.

## SAVE-THE-DATE CARDS

A save-the-date is especially important for destination weddings, as it lets guests know details well in advance. Ideally, you should send out your save-the-dates a year in advance to give guests optimal time to plan.

Save-the-Date DOs and DON'Ts:

DON'T send a save-the-date until you have confirmed your wedding date with your various venues. This always includes a contract and deposit. You don't want circumstances to change after you've sent out the card, especially if your destination changes and guests' have booked their travel.

**DO** send your save-the-date out as soon as your details have been confirmed. The longer your guests have to make arrangements, the more likely they will be able to attend.

**DON'T** send a save-the-date to everyone you intend to invite, only to immediate family and close friends. Once you send a save-the-date to someone, you have to follow up with an invitation. Later you may choose to scale back the wedding day, so include only those on your A list.

**DON'T** get hung up on coordinating your cards with the wedding theme or invitations. Most couples are just beginning to plan at this point

**DO** be inspired by your wedding's location. If you are getting married on an island, use that as a design element. If you are getting married at a vineyard, incorporate wine in your save-the-date. Keep it fun and festive so that guests will get excited about the trip ahead.

**DO** create a wedding website and list the URL on your save-the-date. List preliminary details there so guests can get more information and return for updates.

**DO** send a physical save-the-date card rather than an electronic one. No matter how casual your wedding will be, it is still an important occasion. Your guests will love receiving something in the mail that will remind them of the adventure you are taking together!

# WEDDING WEBSITES

Having a website dedicated solely to information about your wedding might seem a little strange, but I can assure you that this is the norm. All of our couples have a wedding website where they list helpful information regarding travel and, of course, maintain the excitement up to wedding day. There is a lot of information your guests will need to know about your destination wedding, and it would be impossible to include all the information on a save-the-date or wedding invitation. A wedding website helps to answer questions so you are not inundated with emails, phone calls, and text messages asking, "What airport should we fly into again?" You and your sanity will thank me for this later, I promise!

There are several online venues for building your wedding website. Here are a few of my favorites.

- mywedding.com: This website has some great templates (more than 600). You can add photo galleries, link to your registry, and manage your RSVPs. It also has some pretty cool planning elements like budget building and checklists.
- ewedding.com: This website offers options such as a unique domain name, text alerts when guests RSVP, and high-quality website templates. The fully customizable website can be linked to your mobile devices and lets you add a fun "relationship timeline" that tells the story of how you met and got engaged.
- applycouple.com: This website and app offers RSVP tracking, photo sharing, privacy options, travel options, online chat, and more than 500 stylish designs.
- rileygrey.com: Riley Grey has done away with cheesy wedding themes and offers fresh, modern designs. Here you can also manage RSVPs, match your invitation design, accommodate different languages and traditions, and much more.

Test-drive the options to find the best fit. Most of the sites listed above will give you a trial period before you commit to purchasing the service. Once you've chosen a service, put together the information outlined below. Don't worry if you don't have everything together when you send out your save-the-dates. However, make sure your website has all these details once your wedding invitations are mailed:

- Wedding date, time, and the location of your ceremony and reception.
- The story of you: give your guests the "deets" on how you met, where you got engaged, and why you chose this destination for your wedding.
- Additional events: dates, times, and locations for events such as a welcome party, rehearsal dinner, and post-wedding brunch.

- Travel details: including the closest airport to fly into, which airlines fly to your destination and from where, and information on getting from the airport to a hotel or resort. Include any travel requirements such as passport, visa, or health precautions your guests need to take before entering another country.
- Accommodations: any room blocks you've secured and instructions on how to receive those rates, the cost, information about the hotel(s), and their website with contact details.
- Things to do: suggestions for what to do at your wedding destination during guests' downtime. Note places to eat, attractions to visit, and other places your guests may want to check out while on vacation.
- Tips and advice: include a packing list of must-have items such as sunscreen, bug spray, a big floppy hat, and good vibes! Let guests know what they should bring to make their stay comfortable.
- Wedding registry: include links to your wedding registry so guests who would like to buy you a gift can send it directly to your home, rather than bringing it with them. This isn't a call for gifts, as your guests **will** want to buy you something and will want to know what you need or want.
- Pictures: include pictures of the two of you and photographs from the destination, too! Guests will want to see where they're going and where certain events will take place.
- Additional information: include anything else your guests should know as they prepare to jet off to your wedding.
- Thank you: don't forget to thank your guests for being part of your adventure.

## WEDDING INVITATION

Your wedding invitation will be an initial glimpse into what your guests can expect. It is one of the first items your guests will hold in their hands and experience with their senses. Over the years, invitations have transformed from traditional and formal to literally whatever **you** want them to be. I prefer the latter, as it should reflect your personal style.

Invitation designers have become wildly popular, especially for couples who value unique paper goods. Are you someone who dreams about 220lb Crane Lettra card stock and two-color letterpress with gold foil? Do you get giddy when you receive a card with a custom envelope liner? Do you send

out monogrammed, custom thank-you cards to your friends? Do you sweat over the perfectly wrapped gift? Do you know what edge tinting is? If you answered yes to any of the above, you are a lover of paper, and may I be the first to say, welcome to the club! Personally, I love customized paper details and the more luxurious, the better. I appreciate the thought, skill, and tradition involved in making a one-of-a-kind, bespoke wedding invitation.

Some of you may be thinking, "Is she crazy? That doesn't seem like a good investment!" If paper is low on your priority list, consider purchasing a nice invitation from an online retailer. Regardless of whether you're a paper aficionado or just see it as something that will eventually be thrown away, your destination wedding invitation should have these key elements:

- Outer envelope: this contains the entire suite.
- Inner envelope: this is for a more formal occasion and usually has the first name of the guest(s) written on the front.
- Wedding invitation: this is the invitation itself, and it is usually only inviting guests to the ceremony. You may choose to have a secondary card that invites guests to the reception, especially if it is at a different location. Or, you may choose to place both on the main invitation.
- Information card: accommodations, travel arrangements, schedule of events, and your wedding URL where all this information is presented. Never place your wedding website URL on the invitation, no matter how informal the day will be. Also, be sure not to place it on the RSVP card, as that gets mailed back.
- RSVP card: encourage your guests to RSVP on your wedding website in addition to mailing back the card. If you choose to only have guests RSVP digitally, that is okay, but there is something nostalgic about mailed RSVPs, because they are something you reread in the years to come.

If you want to design a more robust invitation suite that could live in the pages of *Martha Stewart Weddings*, the sky's the limit! Let your imagination run wild and hire an invitation designer that gets your aesthetic. The following chapters showcase a lot of paper goodness to inspire you.

Entire books have been written on wedding invitation etiquette. Two such books are *Emily Post's Wedding Etiquette* by Anna Post & Lizzie Post, and *Crane & Co's The Wedding Bluebook* by Steven Feinburg. They will tell you how to properly address an outer envelope and how to word a wedding invitation if your parents, who are hosting the day, are divorced. Certain traditions deserve attention, and when you work with a stationery designer and/or wedding planner, they, too, can advise you on protocol.

Send your destination wedding invitations out well in advance—up to six months ahead, compared to the recommended twelve weeks for a local wedding. You'll want to give guests plenty of time to make travel arrangements.

This will also give you time to wrap up planning, tweak your budget, and finalize your numbers. There are many decisions you'll have to make that can't be determined until you know how many people to expect, so having a guest count three months in advance allows you to make those decisions sooner and avoid stress.

The wedding invitation design is almost always a launch point for other paper details like welcome totes, menu cards, table numbers, bar signs, and thank-you cards. Have fun threading elements of the design throughout your wedding day paper!

Photo
by Joel
Calloway

# 6

## LOGISTICS & WEDDING DAY TIPS

After you've spent endless after-work hours sending emails and making phone calls (and—let's be honest, during working hours, too), and a trip or two to your wedding location, after a few DIY projects gone awry, an argument with your partner over the importance of the perfect napkin fold, and hours of research, worry, and excitement, the big day arrives. All that investment is compressed into one day of joy. It is important that you pay close attention to the logistics and timing of your wedding day events to get the most out of the hours you have.

When you have a wedding in an unfamiliar location, it's easy to misjudge the time it takes to get from point A to B. A wedding planner will help you manage these details, but here are some helpful tips on scheduling your day:

**1** For brides, the day always starts with plugging in curling irons and the flick of powder from a makeup artists' brush. How your day begins will determine how it ends, so start with a solid game plan. Ensure that your beauty team is large enough to handle your bridal party, and when in doubt, hire an extra makeup artist or hair stylist. Consider having your beauty team stay on to provide touch-ups throughout the day, especially if the climate is hot and humid.

**2** For grooms, the day usually starts with a beverage (or two) and breakfast. Assemble your partners-in-crime a few hours ahead of the time you need to be ready so you can enjoy a meal and a beer together. Prepare yourself for a little hazing and some reminiscing about your time as friends. Avoid dangerous activities like rock climbing, surfing, skiing, and any other activity where you can break a bone, lose an eye, or end up at the hospital.

**3** Make sure your hair and makeup are completed thirty minutes before you need to get dressed. This allows for any touch-ups you might require, and also gives you time to get your bearings before you slip into your wedding attire. You can spend that time having a bite to eat or taking a quiet moment to reflect on the beautiful day ahead.

**4** Schedule your photographer and videographer to arrive an hour before hair and makeup is complete so they can capture the final touch-ups.

**5** Let your bridal party get dressed before you do— including your parents. You should be the last person slipping into your gown or fixing your bow tie. You'll get nicer pictures when everyone around you is polished and ready to go, plus, you won't be waiting on that friend who is never ready on time!

**6** If you've hired a bridal dresser, find out when she would like to arrive and ensure that she has a wedding day timeline. They will help everyone get ready, not just you! The next chapter contains more information on the bridal dresser's role and the benefits of having one.

**7** In later chapters, you'll also learn about the importance of a first look—and I would like to reiterate that here. Taking pictures of the two of you, your wedding party, and immediate family members before the ceremony makes great use of time and helps to quell any jitters. Allot yourself a solid two hours for pre-ceremony first-look pictures, starting with just the two of you, then your bridal party, and have immediate family members arrive thirty to forty-five minutes before pictures are scheduled to end. If you have children in your wedding, they should arrive around the same time as your family. Kids lose interest quickly, especially when they have to stand still for pictures. They would rather be running around or twirling in their flower girl dresses.

**8** Hire your transportation to arrive fifteen minutes before you think you'll depart for the wedding venue, just in case you are ready to get the show on the road early! This also includes transportation for your guests. If you are having buses drive your guests to location, tell guests the busses will depart roughly fifteen minutes before their actual departure time. This helps to ensure that no one gets left behind. Having adequate transportation, if needed, to and from all your locations is a must. Don't leave anything to chance or a cab—this is an invitation to unnecessary stress. Pad your transportation time to account for traffic, accidents, and road closures.

**9** List the ceremony time on your invitation earlier than when it is scheduled to begin. If you want to start at 3:30, write 3:00 or 3:15 on the invitation. Guests tend to arrive right at start time, and this will help to ensure there are no stragglers.

**10** Arrive at the ceremony site up to thirty minutes early. If there is a room where you can wait, use that space for final preparations. Otherwise, stay relaxed and cool in your bus or limo with your bridal party.

**11** If you have children in your wedding, be prepared for the unexpected! Embrace the fact that they might get confused, have a meltdown, or do something funny during their walk down the aisle. Enlist someone in the bridal party to keep an eye on them, and have a special treat ready for them at the end of the aisle—it will help encourage them to make it all the way down! And if they don't make it, don't worry—that's just part of being a kid.

**12** Schedule a rehearsal the day before the ceremony. This helps everyone who will stand beside you understand their cues and where they should stand. To make it easy, you can rehearse the ceremony just before your rehearsal dinner—schedule it an hour before additional guests are slated to arrive.

**13** Don't serve alcoholic beverages before the ceremony. There will be plenty of time to pop champagne, and you don't want an over-indulgent guest already at level ten before you walk down the aisle. Instead, offer a refreshing beverage. Cucumber water or peach iced tea are great for warm climates, while warm apple cider is the perfect accompaniment to a fall or winter wedding.

**14** After the ceremony, take a moment for yourselves—just the two of you. You did it! You're married! This might be the only moment in the day where you get to be alone, so take the time to be emotional and excited.

**15** Once you've done that, have your photographer take more pictures of just the two of you. If you opted not to have a first look, now is the time for family photographs. Try not to schedule too many photo locations—if you can, stick to one. The more travel you have to do, especially with a large group, the more time you'll waste waiting around.

**16** After the ceremony, have your guests head straight to the party. A buffer of an hour or two kills the momentum. Guests get confused about where they are supposed to go and what they should do between events.

**17** Try to attend cocktail hour. It is everyone's favorite time, and you can use this hour to mingle with your guests, thank them for coming, and give them huge hugs. Plus, you don't want to miss the delicious food you paid for and the fun signature drink you designed!

**18** Limit the toasts to three or four. At most weddings, a parent or significant family member will open the evening, followed by the maid of honor and then best man. Both of you may choose to say a few words, which guests appreciate. Don't be shy— these are your closest family and friends. Grab the mic and thank them for coming. If you have a lot of people who want to say a few words, you can also have toasts at your welcome party and rehearsal dinner.

**19** Your toasts can be scheduled at the tail end of cocktail hour, once everyone is seated for dinner, or between courses. Most couples want to maximize dancing time, and if that is important, schedule your toasts at the end of cocktail hour or after you've been introduced and have had your first dance. When toasts are scheduled throughout several dinner courses, the dinner service takes much longer than necessary.

**20** Being introduced as a newly married couple is a cause for celebration, and is a nice lead-in to your first dance. You don't need to come in, guns blazing, to "Eye of the Tiger" if that's not your jam. If you want to keep it simple, come in to the beginning of your first dance song.

**21** Speak with your caterer ahead of time to understand how long dinner will take. A buffet or action stations take the least amount of time. Serving a duet plate—two entree items on one dinner plate—will also minimize time in the kitchen. The more courses you have and the more choices you offer, the longer dinner will take. I'm never one to rush dinner if clients want to make that a focal point of the evening; if you feel that way, try to keep it under two hours.

**22** If you want to keep the party energy high all night, cut your cake and twirl around the dance floor with your respective parents as dinner ends. After that formality, you are free to pump for the rest of the night.

**23** Toss your bouquet. It is tradition, after all, and there will be some single women at your wedding. The garter toss is up to you.

**24** If you leave your wedding before it ends, gather your guests for a proper send-off. You can switch into another outfit, á la Jackie O, and jump into a waiting car amid a petal toss.

Part of a well-managed wedding day includes communicating timing to your bridal party. Put together a timeline that includes the time busses will arrive, when the ceremony will start, when specific bridal party members and family will give toasts, and what time your dad should put his jacket back on for your dance together. People feel better when they know what is expected of them.

# 7

## WHEN ALL ELSE FAILS, ELOPE!

Maybe you are at the beginning stages of planning your destination wedding and the cost is daunting. Perhaps family dynamics have you teetering on the edge. It could also be that you don't want a big wedding, and you'd rather it just be the two of you. If that is the case, consider eloping!

This is something I have personal experience with, since I eloped with my husband. We had an intimate wedding in which just two people witnessed us exchanging our vows. Words escape me to describe how magical, personal, and romantic our wedding was— it was the perfect option for us. You can have a gorgeous wedding, even if it's just the two of you!

Elopements don't have to mean the drive-through wedding chapel in Vegas; they can have all the bells and whistles of your dream wedding, without the cost and stress. Many couples consider luxury elopements in lieu of the big wedding. You can still wear the gown of your dreams, carry a magnificent bouquet of flowers, and dine on a seven-course meal prepared just for you in a magical setting. With an elopement, the sky really is the limit on how extravagant or understated your wedding can be.

I know from my own experience that the one obstacle to elopements is others' expectations. Some people close to you will be upset that they didn't have the opportunity to see you get married. Their disappointment comes from a place of love, because they want to be included in the celebration. So, if you choose to elope, you can always have a celebratory party later in your hometown and invite all your family and friends. This is also true for a smaller destination wedding that not everyone can attend. You will have an opportunity to celebrate with all those who love you and share the gorgeous images of your intimate, romantic elopement.

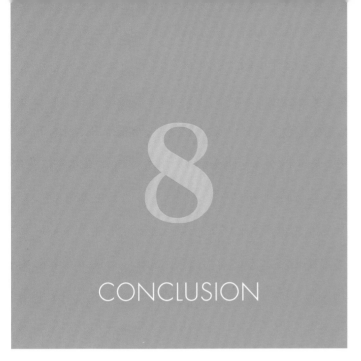

# 8

## CONCLUSION

If I were to give just one piece of advice, it would be this: Relax. Breathe. Enjoy every second of your wedding day. Don't expect everything to be perfect, because nothing is perfect and something **will** go awry. Laugh about it, hold your partner's hand, look around at all the people who love you, and realize that is what matters. Your journey together starts right here, and every day after this day will be one you step into together. I say this to all my couples on their wedding day and I want to say this to you, too: may you be surrounded by the love you feel on this day, every day that you spend together.

"Fashion is not something that exists in dresses only. Fashion is in the sky, in the street, FASHION HAS TO DO WITH IDEAS, THE WAY WE LIVE, WHAT IS HAPPENING."

—Coco Chanel

# Selecting DESTINATION WEDDING Fashion

## Beth Lindsay Chapman

The attire for your destination wedding sets the tone for your big day. It should reflect your individual style as well as the aesthetic and formality level of the wedding.

## FINDING YOUR WEDDING DAY STYLE

The first step in finding your wedding day style is to identify your individual style. Think about the clothing you put on every day. Is it classic, modern, eclectic, vintage, or bohemian? That's what you will be most comfortable wearing.

When choosing a wedding aesthetic, inspiration can come from anywhere. Browse through Pinterest, Instagram, bridal blogs, coffee table books, and bridal and fashion magazines. You might even find it in a romantic city, a movie, the colors of a sunset, a favorite pair of shoes, words from a romantic poem, or the colors in a painting. The key is to find something to act as a road map as you plan. Your attire should follow suit and reflect that overall vision.

Use your wedding venue as a muse for your wedding fashion. The level of formality, colors, and even the fabric should be influenced by where your wedding is taking place.

Take cues from the larger context as well: your destination's history, culture, and architecture can all help you plan a cohesive wedding ensemble.

The architecture of your wedding destination can inspire your wedding gown.

# SHOPPING FOR YOUR WEDDING GOWN

Selecting a wedding gown is one of the first steps a bride takes on the journey of her engagement. Finding the perfect gown is exciting, but can sometimes be confusing and overwhelming. These tips will help to make the experience memorable, enjoyable, and lead to the gown of your dreams.

**1** Secure your wedding date and venue. Your gown decision will be much easier to make if you can envision yourself wearing it in a particular setting. Consider the climate and your ability to transport the gown.

**2** Set a realistic budget. Your budget should not only include an allocation for the gown, but also accessories (bra, veil, jewelry, and shoes), alterations, and gown cleaning and preservation after the wedding. It is very important to articulate your budget to the sales associate. You don't want to fall in love with something that doesn't fit your budget. My best advice is to avoid trying on gowns that fall outside of your budget! That is a recipe for disappointment.

**3** Do your research. Before you start to shop, research bridal salons that carry designers that meet your taste level and budget. Think about the types of stores where you shop for everyday clothes. If you are a department store shopper, a large bridal salon with a large selection may be the right fit. If you prefer to shop in small boutiques, a more intimate bridal store will likely be a better choice.

Visit the store's website to ensure that the selection and price range meets your needs. It is also helpful to read bridal blogs to find out what other brides-to-be have to say about the stores that you plan to visit.

**4** Plan ahead. Call to schedule an appointment at least one week in advance. This allows the bridal store to give you one-on-one attention. It takes four to six months to produce a wedding gown, so you should begin shopping for your gown at least nine months in advance of the wedding to allow time for alterations once the gown arrives.

**5** Limit opinions. This is a momentous and joyous time in your life, so naturally you want to share it with your family and friends. Be cautious, however, of bringing a large group with you. Too many opinions can be detrimental to making a decision. My advice is to shop with one or two close family members or friends who understand and respect your personal style. Once you have selected your gown, you can invite your bridesmaids and other family members to one of your fittings.

Consider others' opinions, but keep in mind that, ultimately, you know yourself best. Your opinion is truly the only one that matters. It is your day and you are the one wearing the gown.

**6** Communicate. Bring photographs of styles you like to the appointment and articulate your vision and budget to the sales associate. Don't be afraid to speak up if you don't like a gown detail. It can often be customized to give you just what you want. Before making the final decision, be sure you understand the store policies regarding the deposit and alterations fees. Let the sales associate know about your destination wedding so she can make suggestions for transporting the gown and steaming or pressing it upon arrival.

**7** Stay true to your style. This is a continuous theme, as it is the most important aspect of choosing wedding attire. Don't use your wedding as an opportunity to make a fashion statement. Your gown should flatter your best physical assets, reflect the formality level and overall aesthetic of your venue, and most importantly, reflect your personality. You want to still look like yourself on your wedding day . . . just an enhanced version!

**8** Keep an open mind. Trust the sales associate you are working with. If they are good at what they do, they will listen to your vision and suggest gowns to try on. Even if you don't like the way a gown looks on the hanger, try it on! It could be the gown of your dreams!

**9** Don't be alarmed by the size. Bridal sizing is different from ready-to-wear sizing. The wedding industry is based on tradition and many of today's bridal designer size charts are created from European size charts from fifty years ago. In some cases, a bridal gown is two sizes larger than you normally wear. Allow the bridal store to take your measurements and compare them to the size chart in order to select your appropriate size. Gowns are rarely made to your exact measurements. If any of your measurements fall between sizes, it is safer to go up one size. It is easier for a seamstress to take in a gown than to let it out.

> A gown can be altered up to two sizes while still maintaining the integrity of the design. Even if you are planning to lose weight, order the size you measure at the time of purchase and alter the gown once it arrives. Never order a gown based on the size that you plan to be at the wedding. Remember, the size is just a number!

**10** The perfect gown starts with the perfect foundation. Undergarments are called the foundation for a reason: they make all the difference in a gown's fit. After your gown is purchased, take time to select the perfect undergarments. Shop in a location that specializes in foundations so you are sized correctly.

- Select a bra or bustier that has a lower back than that of the gown so the bra is not visible.
- If your bra has lace, texture, or boning, make sure it is not visible through the gown. If you can see the bra's bottom edge through the fabric, try wearing a control top undergarment and tuck the bottom of the bra into it.

- If your gown is a column silhouette or made of a lightweight fabric, make sure your undergarments give you enough support and that there are no noticeable seams or panty lines.
- If you are getting married in a tropical location, consider wearing a body shaper under your gown. This will provide an extra layer between you and your gown and will absorb perspiration.

**11** Alterations. Alterations are truly a process. It will take time to sculpt the gown to fit your body perfectly. When purchasing your gown, factor in a minimum of two months for alterations. You can expect an average of three alteration appointments to get a perfect fit. Select your shoes and undergarments before your first appointment, because it is impossible to ensure a proper fit without those elements. If you are losing weight, don't begin the alterations process until your weight is stable.

**12** Create the look. Accessories should never be an afterthought. They are the finishing touches that tie your wedding day look together. If your venue and décor have a vintage feel, search for vintage accessories or ones with that aesthetic. If a color is playing an important role in your wedding, consider carrying that color into your bridal party accessories. The color should be subtle—a little goes a long way! You can incorporate color into your bridal accessories with a colored shoe (or just the sole of the shoe providing a pop of color), a colorful clutch, or even a cardigan or wrap if the evening is chilly. Later we'll discuss how to incorporate a touch of color into a groom's attire.

Shoe selection is important in a destination wedding. Consider the ceremony and photo portrait locations. If your destination has cobblestone streets or grass, you may want to consider a wedge heel, which provides height but also stability.

If you are getting married on a beach, but want to change to a heel for your reception, have the seamstress hem the dress to your heel height. Most likely you will have to hold the front of your gown up on the beach anyway. It is more important that you are able to walk and dance without tripping during your reception.

When selecting your finishing touches, ask yourself if you want the accessories to be the statement or if you want them to simply complement the gown. Either way, they should reflect your style and the overall wedding aesthetic.

**13** Protect your investment. Although you will wear your gown only once, it holds many memories and should be properly cleaned and protected after the wedding. Research companies that specialize in gown cleaning and preservation—don't rely on your local dry cleaner. Often the bridal store where you purchased your gown will offer this service. Select a company that uses an anti-sugar cleaning treatment and acid-free materials in the preservation box. These processes ensure that the gown will not discolor or deteriorate over time.

**14** Enjoy the experience. The most important tip in shopping for your gown is to have fun! How often in life will you be able to try on beautiful gowns and be treated like a princess? Enjoy every minute of it! The key is to make sure you are working with a bridal salon that maximizes your bridal shopping experience and makes you feel comfortable as you make your decision.

## TO VEIL OR NOT TO VEIL?

For a bride, a veil is a very personal decision. Keep your ceremony environment in mind when considering this option. If you are getting married in a windy location such as on the beach or on top of a mountain, a veil, particularly a long one, might not be the best choice. Although a blowing veil can be beautiful in photographs, it can be distracting during your ceremony. If you want to wear a veil, opt for a veil with lace or beaded trim. The novelty detail will add a little weight. Also, make sure your maid of honor is ready to remove your veil for you if it becomes distracting during the ceremony.

Having a trim on your veil that adds a bit of weight, like lace, helps to keep it from blowing off in a windy location.

A reception dress is a way to change up your look. A gown that may have been too risqué for your ceremony could be the perfect choice for dancing the night away.

# SECOND LOOK

It has become popular for both brides and grooms to opt for a second look for their reception. If you are a bride, choosing a reception dress allows you to change into something more comfortable for dancing. If you are hosting a destination wedding in tropical location, a second dress might be a welcome relief from the heat. A reception dress is also a way to change the sensibility of your look. It allows you to select a more conservative or classic look for your ceremony and then unveil a sexier look for the reception.

If you love color but do not want to use it on your wedding gown, consider a quick change into a fun cocktail dress in the wedding's accent color. Be sure to check out the second looks used in our inspiration shoots in Behind the Design.

Grooms can change up their reception look as well. Though I've always been a fan of the classic white dinner jacket for the reception, recently I've become enamored with adding subtle color. Consider switching out your black tux jacket for a navy or gray one with a black lapel, or search for a tweed or patterned jacket in the wedding colors. This is a great way to show your personality.

Second looks are not just for the bride! Changing from a classic black tuxedo jacket to a white dinner jacket gives the groom a new look for the reception.

Hiring a wedding dresser is an insurance policy against fashion mishaps.

# INVESTING IN A BRIDAL DRESSER

Bridal dressers like a fashion insurance policy for your wedding day. They are hired not only to dress you, but to solve any fashion emergencies. A bridal dresser will steam your gown, help you get dressed, and ensure that you are picture-perfect for your first look and portraits. They will also fluff the gown and veil prior to your walk down the aisle and bustle your train before you are introduced into the reception. If you have a reception dress, they can also be invaluable in preparing and dressing you in your second look. A bridal dresser is often an event planner and photographer's best friend, as they allow the planner to focus on the details and timeline, rather than on fashion issues. They also act as a stylist to ensure that every fashion and beauty detail is perfectly executed, which makes for better photographs. If you are the type of bride who wants a little extra pampering on your wedding day or does not want to burden your mother or maid of honor, this service may be a good choice.

# BRIDAL BEAUTY

After you have selected your gown and accessories, schedule a beauty trial to explore complementary hair and beauty styles. You may want to do this earlier on the day of a gown fitting appointment so you can see the entire look.

This may be difficult for a destination wedding, although you can research beauty professionals near the venue and see examples of their work prior to booking. Make sure that your hair and makeup artists are clear on your vision and ask to see examples of similar looks they've created. I suggest scheduling your hair and makeup appointment just prior to the rehearsal dinner or civil ceremony, so there are no surprises on your wedding day, and you'll look fabulous at these events. If you don't want your hair to be the same at your rehearsal dinner and wedding, have the stylist practice the wedding day look so you are confident in it, and then change it up slightly for the rehearsal.

If you are hiring a professional makeup team, always have a trial.

If you are nervous about leaving your beauty trial until several days before your wedding, have a beauty trial at home and ask for a detailed lesson on how to recreate the look yourself.

Again, be cognizant of your environment. If you are getting married in a windy or humid location, select an up do. In a warm climate, you may need additional makeup products such as SPF and primer. As always, let the professionals you have hired guide you.

# DRESSING FOR A WARM-WEATHER DESTINATION

Fabric weight is an important factor to consider if you are tying the knot in a tropical location. Fabrics well-suited to a hot, humid climate include:

- Silk organza—a sheer, lightweight fabric woven from silk. This fabric lends itself beautifully to an A-line or ball gown silhouette, allowing you to have a princess look without adding weight from the fabric.

Organza lends itself beautifully to an A-line or ball gown silhouette, creating a princess look without adding weight.

Chiffon is a wonderful option for a tropical location, as it will blow gracefully in the wind.

- Chiffon—a flowy, sheer fabric woven from silk or polyester. It is delicate and will blow gracefully in the wind.
- Tulle—a sheer, net fabric woven from silk or nylon fibers. This fabric travels well. Similar to organza, tulle drapes beautifully in a fuller silhouette, allowing you to have a lightweight ball gown that will not wrinkle.
- Lace—a traditional fabric, often woven in a floral pattern. In a tropical location, consider a lightweight lace, like Chantilly lace—a delicate, floral handmade lace named after the region of France where it originated. I love lace in traditional venues, like a castle or in a European city, as it has a classic, Old World feel—and it resists wrinkles.

Tulle travels well and drapes beautifully in a fuller silhouette, allowing you to have a ball gown that will not wrinkle and will be light to wear.

Lace is a good choice for a destination wedding, as it resists wrinkling in transit.

The groom should choose natural-fiber fabrics such as cotton, linen, or a silk blend.

For grooms who prefer to not wear a tux or suit, a white shirt, no tie, and crisp trousers look elegant. If you prefer a traditional look for the ceremony but want to be more casual at the reception, wear a suit for the ceremony, and then replace the jacket with a vest (I love this look with or without a tie). This look is tailored, but still weather appropriate. Above all, the couple's clothing should share the same level of formality at the ceremony.

Natural-fiber fabrics such as cotton, linen, or a silk blend keep a groom cool in a warm climate.

Brides think they need to avoid a ball gown or fuller silhouette if they are getting married in a warm climate. This is not the case, as long as the fabric is lightweight. Another option is to wear a fuller silhouette for the ceremony and then change into a sheath or short gown for the reception. If you can't bear to take off your gown, consider a detachable train or a full overskirt you can remove for the reception.

# WHAT TO WEAR WHEN YOU ELOPE

When you elope, any fashion goes!

Eloping is all about you and your fiancé, so anything goes from a fashion perspective. You may decide to whisk away to Paris for the weekend and wear a traditional wedding gown to exchange vows in front of the Eiffel tower, or wear a short, flirty dress to be married by a justice of the peace in a vineyard in Napa Valley. Wear what makes you feel beautiful, and you can't go wrong!

# PERSONALIZING THE GROOM'S ATTIRE

Who says the bride gets to have all the fashion fun? It's becoming more popular for the groom's attire to reflect his personality and the wedding colors.

- Dinner jacket: It is common practice to change from a black tux jacket into a white dinner jacket for the reception. But what about changing into a patterned or colored jacket?
- Touches of color: If you are having a custom suit or tuxedo made for the wedding, it is a nice touch to have the lining of the jacket made in one of the wedding colors. While you're at it, have the tailor embroider your wedding date on the inside.
- Make a statement with socks: Socks are another fun way to inject personality into the groom's ensemble. Perhaps it's a pop of color, a stripe, or even the logo of a favorite sports team.
- Fun with pocket squares: A tie is often used to add color to the groom or groomsmen's look. As an alternative, use a colorful pocket square. A classic black tux with a pop of color or

Changing into a patterned or colored jacket is another way for the groom to vary his look for the reception.

Boutonnières can be a way to incorporate a family heirloom, like your grandmother's hat pin.

Have your florist create a floral pocket square instead of a boutonnière.

pattern in the pocket square can add whimsy to each guy's look. Have fun with this! Mix and match the patterns so that each member of the bridal party has a different look.

- Boutonnières: Gone are the days where the groom has a single rose pinned to his lapel. I love when grooms turn this tradition on its head! Have your floral designer create a floral pocket square in lieu of a boutonnière. Or, instead of using a traditional flower, bring an element of your wedding environment to the lapel—perhaps the leaf of a tropical plant, a small piece of evergreen with an acorn, or a succulent. Boutonnières can also be a way to incorporate a family heirloom. Pin your grandmother's hat pin into the floral motif or have a fabric flower made from the tweed of your father's wedding suit.

# ATTENDANTS' ATTIRE

The rules for attendants' attire have changed. Bridal party outfits are no longer expected to match. I think it's refreshing when couples allow their attendants to choose a dress or suit that flatters them. In a destination wedding, where color and texture often play a key role, it's nice to mix and match bridesmaid silhouettes, colors, and fabrics and to vary the color of groomsmen's suits or the pattern of their tie or pocket square.

# GUEST ATTIRE

We've come a long way from "black tie optional." More couples are making suggestions for what their guests should wear. For a tropical destination, it might be fun to invite guests to dress all in white (it makes for gorgeous photos on the beach). Or if your wedding is in the evening in a romantic setting, perhaps you request that your guests don something that sparkles! Theme dressing sets the tone and gets the guests excited for the wedding. If you don't want to dictate fashion for the big day, you might suggest attire for the rehearsal dinner instead.

Have fun by suggesting attire for your guests on the invitation.

# FASHION OPTIONS FOR SAME SEX COUPLES

Just as for heterosexual couples, it is important for each partner to choose the attire that reflects his or her own style, in keeping with the tone of the wedding.

Two grooms: I believe each groom should have an individual look. If the wedding is formal and both grooms will be wearing classic black tuxes, opt for subtle differences, such as varying lapel shapes or wearing different patterned pocket squares or bow ties. The key is that although you are dressed differently, the level of formality is the same.

Boutonnières are another way to personalize and differentiate your look. Each groom can wear a flower that has significance to him, or incorporate a family heirloom into the floral motif.

Two brides: I recommend that each bride select an ensemble that shows off her individual aesthetic, rather than trying to match a look. This could mean anything from an elaborate ball gown, to an elegant sheath, to a tailored suit. Again, keep the level of formality consistent.

For same-sex weddings, each bride or groom should select an ensemble that shows off their personal style.

# TRAVELING WITH YOUR WEDDING ATTIRE

One of the most nerve-wracking aspects of traveling to a destination wedding is making sure that your wedding attire arrives safely. I never recommend shipping your gown; it is always safest to travel with it. Ask your airline if there is room to store a garment bag in first class or in a flight attendant closet.

If you are traveling with a very large wedding gown, here is fun tip—vacuum seal it! Turn the gown inside out, place it in a large vacuum seal bag intended for a comforter, and remove the air. This will allow you to fit it into a suitcase. When you arrive at the destination, hang the gown immediately. You will be surprised at how few wrinkles it has! Be sure that there is a steamer available for a final pressing on the wedding day.

Some people say that what you wear for your wedding is not significant, as you only wear it one day. I believe the significance lies in the fact that you have hand-selected this ensemble for this meaningful day in your life. You have taken the time to alter it to perfection and selected accessories to complement it. It is a garment that will hold meaning to you every time you look at photographs. The fact that you wear it for one day **is** what makes it so special.

*Happy shopping!*

"The real voyage of discovery consists not in seeking new landscapes, BUT IN HAVING NEW EYES"

—Marcel Proust

# Photographing Your DESTINATION WEDDING

## Carla Ten Eyck

*A*fter everyone has gone home, tans have faded, and passports have been filled and re-issued, wedding photographs are all that's left of your big day—and they are passed on to generations beyond your own. Sadly, I can't tell you how often I've been told that my bride or groom's parent passed away not long after their wedding, and that the photographs I took were their last. I often reflect on this while shooting a wedding, as my own last complete family portrait was taken at my wedding in 1999.

## IDENTIFY THE STYLE OF PHOTOGRAPHY YOU LIKE

The first step in hiring a photographer is to decide what kind of photography you like. Are you into dramatic, staged portraits, or is a fly-on-the-wall documentary approach

more your style? Do you want a mix of both? Do you love soft, flattering natural light or dramatic, warm light with deeper shadows? Do you love seeing lots of little details, or wide, epic landscapes? If you aren't sure, talk to your photographer about his or her style. Browsing through sites such as Pinterest can help you identify your preferences. I have found that talking it through helps my clients understand the things they like about photography but may not have had the language to explain.

# FIND A PHOTOGRAPHER

Once you have figured out your photography aesthetic, ask your planner to recommend compatible photographers. Chemistry is important, too, since a destination wedding goes far beyond the typical eight-hour shoot. Destination weddings are intimate and intense, and your relationship with the photographer can make or break your experience. When I meet with clients, I stress this above all else. Will they feel comfortable working with my team over a multi-day event, which may become stressful at times?

Another way to find photographers is to check with your venue coordinator, or do a Google image search of the property. See what photographers come up and visit their websites. Again, you can also use Pinterest by typing in your venue or locale. If you know people who have gotten married at your venue, ask them for referrals. They may suggest people to hire, or to avoid.

# CONSIDER AN
# ENGAGEMENT SESSION

How can you tell if your photographer is the right fit for you? One option, if your budget allows, is to hire your photographer for an engagement session. An engagement session generally happens after you become engaged and set a date for your wedding. It's a wonderful way to "interview" the photographer to see how well you work together. If you are using someone local, this can work out fabulously.

If the photographer is based at your destination, consider flying him or her in to see how well you work together. If your schedules or budget don't allow for this, consider doing a mini session (fifteen to thirty minutes) during your rehearsal dinner when the light is ideal. This way you can get a feel for how your photographer communicates with you and gives you direction so that your wedding pictures are not the first time

you are working together. I always tell my clients that the first few minutes of any session are kind of a "getting to know you" period, and it is normal to feel awkward and a little uncomfortable before you settle into the flow of the session. If time is tight during the wedding day, I cannot emphasize a small pre-shoot enough—it helps everyone feel comfortable more quickly on the wedding day!

# DOES YOUR PHOTOGRAPHER NEED DESTINATION EXPERIENCE?

During the initial meeting, ask how many destination weddings he or she has photographed and how many additional photographers and assistants they would bring along. It is never a good idea to photograph a wedding alone. Regardless of the number of guests, there could be simultaneous events that need to be covered. I once photographed a wedding in Scotland that had only sixty-five guests, but a staff of 250 was working the event because there was so much to do. Many times, I am doing portraits while cocktail hour is underway, and the only way cocktails can be covered is with the help of another photographer. Other things to consider are assistants, which can be lifesavers. For beach events, I often need a non-shooting assistant to hold my bags and help change the lenses, since sand is the nemesis of photography gear. The bottom line is to be super-transparent about the timing of events and trust your photographer to staff the event accordingly. Your planner will be an amazing resource for this—I usually work with the wedding planner to determine the appropriate staffing level.

# WHAT COVERAGE OPTIONS DOES THE PHOTOGRAPHER OFFER?

Does your photographer offer multi-day coverage? In my opinion you will want this since there is so much to photograph at a destination wedding. Find out how much hourly coverage they suggest for each event. You don't need every minute documented. Consider inviting the photographer(s) to each event, pay them to be "on" for two or three hours, and then allow them to join the party. That way, if something amazing happens they are there, but they don't have to be "on" the entire time and over-shooting each little thing. This also gives them the freedom to recharge before each day's event. You definitely want a well-rested photographer each day, especially if there is a time zone change or the weather is hot.

How do you decide which events to have photographed? My recommendation is to have your rehearsal dinner covered for at least an hour or two; this gives the photographers a chance to acquaint themselves with the key players. Obviously, they will cover the wedding day and can determine what hours are best depending on event timing.

# THE FIRST LOOK

Some couples who have a destination wedding opt not to have "first look" portraits taken right before the wedding ceremony, but rather to have a portrait session the day after the wedding, when there is not as much time pressure. However, I still recommend doing a first look, especially if you are not scheduling a day-after portrait session, as it allows you to get right to the reception rather than shooting after the ceremony. First looks also help to ease any nerves about seeing your fiancé before the wedding. And why not do it while you're at your best? What if the weather doesn't cooperate the next day, or someone spills red wine on your dress during the reception?

# POST-WEDDING DAY
# PORTRAIT SESSION

A post-wedding photo shoot allows you to have a whole day to relax and have fun getting photographed in your wedding outfits. Your photographer can determine the best time of day depending on the light and the local backdrops you've identified for pictures. If you plan on several locations, make sure you pack food and drinks for everyone, since nothing can derail a portrait session more quickly than a thirsty or hungry couple (or photographer!). Grab some ice, a cooler, and some beers and sammies, but don't forget to bring your lipstick for touch-ups! Make sure to check the local calendar for events that could either interfere or add local color to your pictures. A parade or festival could be an awesome place to go poke around in your wedding dress for some really fun images.

# TRUST YOUR PHOTOGRAPHER

I am going to say this again: trust your photographer! Let the team choose locations that speak to them. I know from experience that when I am super-excited by a space, I can create some killer images for the couple because my whole creative mojo is into it! You may not necessarily see what their vision is, but remember you hired them for the way they see the world. Sometimes when I get a great idea, I like to explain my vision to my clients, which sometimes includes yelling and hollering and just being super-excited about it! This rubs off on my couple and adds to the energy of the session. I am a strong believer in giving feedback to my clients while I am photographing; it is a true game changer!

# HOW CAN YOU TELL IF YOUR PHOTOGRAPHER HANDLES STRESS WELL?

I am sure this goes without saying, but hire someone who you feel relaxed with and who reacts well under pressure. There will inevitably be things that change on the spot and you definitely want someone who can roll with the changes. During interviews, notice how they are on the phone or Skype. Try FaceTiming or doing a Google hangout with them via video so you can see their mannerisms. Are they amiable and easy to chat with? How do they react to your questions? Are they stressed? You have to evaluate how relaxed you think they would really be in another country, out of their element, with things changing on the fly. Trust your gut and let your comfort level be a strong determining factor in your decision.

# WILL YOUR PHOTOGRAPHER SCOUT LOCATIONS BEFORE THE EVENT?

Don't let a photographer's familiarity with the destination always be a factor in your hiring decision. One of my superhero skills is being able to find nooks to shoot in anywhere and assess the light on the fly. I pride myself on this! That said, I like to arrive at least one day early so I can adjust to any time zone changes and scout locations.

Although it adds expense, ask whether your photographer prefers to arrive a day early to scope out the terrain and light.

How do your photographers see light? If they define themselves as natural/available light photographers, as I do, how does that translate to night photographs? This portrait was made with only available light, which included the headlights of a car as it drove by the cafe and happened to light the couple perfectly, without spoiling the street ambience of Montmartre.

This bride is sitting elegantly in a window—a shot captured by moving tables and chairs.

To fully tell the story of this Paris destination, I asked street performers to create a cut-out of my couple. I love her reaction as she sees the finished product!

Use local attractions and landscapes to capture the flavor of your destination. Paris is known for its romantic Pont des Artes bridge, where lovers place locks on the bridge as a sign of their undying love. What an epic backdrop for a portrait of two people in love.

# WHAT TO ASK FOR IN YOUR PHOTOGRAPHY PACKAGE

Ask to have an album included in the package quote. You can do a multi-volume set with photographic prints mounted on a thin but non-bendable board. This is also called a flush mounted album. Or you can opt for a coffee table–style album with more flexible pages. If you've had several events photographed, a coffee table album works best to tell the story of the event. It can also be freeing and wonderful to let your photographer choose the images to create a story. He or she can weave details, scene-setters, portraits, and candid moments together to tell the story in a way that you wouldn't necessarily see if you chose each image. This is how I do most albums, and I have to tell you, my clients love it!

# DON'T FORGET—PHOTOGRAPHY IS AN INVESTMENT

Don't be cheap—destination weddings are not just an eight-hour affair for your photographer. In addition to the wedding day, there might be a welcome party to shoot, a rehearsal dinner, brunch, and portraits taken off-property. This can result in amazing photo ops. Don't skimp and miss out on some of the best pictures you may get of your guests relaxing and getting to know each other! The cost of photography may offset the savings of having a smaller destination affair, so work with your planner to budget accordingly. The memories are what you will have when it's all over and everyone has gone home, but your images will live forever.

# PALM BEACH

### Inspired by

### Pineapples & Stripes

Welcome to Palm Beach, a Floridian city known for its preppy, tropical style. From the historic Chesterfield Hotel, to the pristine white sand beaches dotted with striped umbrellas, to a window-shopping stroll along the famous palm tree-lined Worth Avenue, Palm Beach embodies a classic style with a modern, colorful twist!

This styled shoot took place in an industrial blank slate that was converted to a wedding venue. We incorporated bold patterns made up of pineapples and stripes with bright color pops of coral and orange. We sprinkled in a touch of Hollywood regency, clean white backdrops, and gilded pineapples, and suddenly we were transported to Palm Beach. The most luxurious part of this story is the floral tablescape runner, which drips down the edge of the table in a colorful array of texture and decadence.

Now, mix up a piña colada and let's take a trip into this modern, stylish wedding.

carla & ad
11825 SUNSET CIRCL
TELLURIDE, COLORA
8 1 4 3

TOGETHER with their FAMILIES

riley
&
joshua

INVITE YOU TO THEIR
FUN-FILLED WEDDING EXTRAVAGANZA

SATURDAY 26 SEPTEMBER

{TWENTY FIFTEEN}
four o'clock in the afternoon

THE LOADING DOCK
375 Fairfield Avenue • Stamford, Connecticut

# WOoO! WHoO!

WE CAN'T WAIT TO CELEBRATE WITH YOU!
KINDLY REPLY BY AUGUST 12

M

But of course, dear!

With tears, no.

13

*riley & joshua*

438 SILVER BROOK ROAD, WESTPORT, CONNECTICUT

**06880**

WHAT'S THAT?

YOU WANNA KNOW WHERE THE PARTY'S AT?
VISIT OUR SITE FOR ALL THE INSIDE SCOOP!

www·rileyandjoshua·com

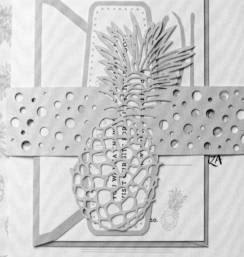

TOGETHER with their FAMILIES

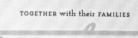

THE LOADING DOCK
375 Fairfield Avenue • Stamford, Connecticut

"The *Lilly* girl is always full of surprises.
She lives every day like it's a celebration,
never has a dull moment,
and makes every hour happy hour."

—Lilly Pulitzer

MOLLY BIERMAN

4

riley ♥ joshua

taste & toast

**FIRST COURSE**
FLAMED LOBSTER RAVIOLI
ragout of butternut squash bolognese, lobster and
sage atina a bed of broccoli rabe, roasted

**Second COURSE**
THE GOLDEN CAESAR SALAD
crisper lettuce wittuce, shaved parmigiano
ad lemon arugula and arugula, croutons
and lemon vinaigrette crispy prosciutto flatbread

**ENTRÉE**
GRILLED STEAKHOUSE FILET
beef and fire, caramelized onions, duck fat
potato and fire, caramelized onions, duck fat
springly spinach, middleweis creamed spinach

**DESSERT**
chocolate tart
gently dark
gently whipped cream
gently whipped cream

PINEAPPLE
JUICE + ICED CAKE
VODKA

CHEERS!

PINEAPPLE
Juice

PINEAPPLE
JUICE

TROPICAL TRAIL MIX

PINEAPPLE Juice

RILEY & JOSHUA'S WEDDING WEEKEND

Hello friends and family! We are beyond excited to
have you here for our happy celebration. We've
been counting down the days and can't believe it's
already the big weekend. Yay!

It means the world to us that you are here. Thank
you for making the journey for us. We are truly
blessed to have you in our lives and to have you here
for our biggest moment. This weekend wouldn't be
the same without you and we can't wait to celebrate
with you. Now let's get this party started!

PINEAPPLE
JUICE + ICED CAKE
VODKA = PINEAPPLE
UPSIDE-DOWN
CAKE SHOT

POP.
{FIZZ}
CLINK!

THE WEDDING
CELEBRATION
OF
riley
& joshua

The twenty-sixth of September
{TWENTY FIFTEEN}

THE LOADING DOCK
Stamford, Connecticut

# BEHIND THE DESIGN

## Theme

We had fun with this shoot and gave the classic style of Palm Beach a twist while still keeping the integrity of the destination. We swapped out the signature Palm Beach tropical leaves with pineapples and used a stripe motif along with the bold colors the destination is known for.

Here are three design ideas from this shoot:

**Use one design element in several ways:** Since the pineapple was a big focus, it was used as a recurring design element. A recurring design element allows you to thread one idea throughout the entire day in interesting ways. The pineapple appeared in everything from the groom's bow-tie to the napkin at each place setting. We even designed a signature drink around the pineapple! Find unique places to infuse your bespoke design elements to make them stand out.

**Design unexpected areas:** Every part of your wedding is an opportunity to think about how you want it to look and feel. Let your bar areas become a statement piece for the evening, like the ones we designed around this Palm Beach theme. Their sequin panels are the same fabric as our chandeliers and the bar backs are filled with pink champagne and colorful flowers.

**Get colorful:** Don't be afraid of color—embrace it! Long gone are the days of the white wedding, as beautiful as it is. Choose the colors you love most. Don't shy away from mixing bright colors such as the orange, coral, and fuschia we used in this shoot.

## Fashion

The fashion inspiration for this shoot came from the things Palm Beach is known for: color, personality, and whimsy. With all of the dramatic details involved, it was important to select a wedding gown that had enough charm to make its own statement. The tone-on-tone striped Hayley Paige wedding gown did just that! We injected small pops of coral into the bride and groom accessories and the maid's dress to incorporate the signature color. Sometimes, more is more—especially when you are stepping away from tradition.

**Bride:** The reception dress should follow the aesthetic of the wedding gown or encompass the event's overall feel. In this case, a mini dress with a dramatic back bow has the same preppy, whimsical feel as the wedding gown.

A statement necklace can be a great way to introduce personality and color. This is also a great way to change up your look for the reception without changing your dress. A bride can transform her look for the party by removing her veil and adding a dramatic accessory such as a statement necklace or beaded sash.

**Groom:** A little color goes a long way in groom's attire. Socks are a fun way to inject color and personality.

If you have identified a signature element or pattern for your wedding, don't be afraid to subtly incorporate it into your fashion. For this shoot, the pineapple motif, designed by Coral Pheasant Stationery and Design for the invitation's envelope liner, was printed on cotton fabric used to make the groom's bow tie. This subtle detail adds a touch of whimsy and provides a consistent design thread.

**Attendants' attire:** Don't shy away from pattern. My fashion inspiration for this shoot was stripes. The bold stripe in the bridesmaid dress complements the subtle tonal stripe of the wedding gown. Rather than competing, the two complement each other beautifully.

## Paper

We had fun with paper—whether it was the custom, laser- cut pineapple belly band that held all the paper elements together, or the playful typography used in everything from the RSVP card to the bar signs. Paper allows you to fully customize a series of elements with textures, color, motifs, and patterns.

**Save-the-date cards:** Save-the-dates are the first encounter guests have with your wedding. A pineapple-shaped card in yellow stock is the perfect introduction to a fun weekend in Palm Beach.

**Invitations:** The invitation combines all our colors, from the soft pink typography to the orange stripes on the envelope. We created a custom pineapple envelope liner and reused the pattern on custom napkins. Since this wedding was not formal, we used playful language on the RSVP card that said, "Woo-hoo, we can't wait to celebrate with you!"

**Ceremony program:** Your ceremony program is the perfect place to design something both beautiful and meaningful. A laser-cut pineapple and confetti cover flips up to reveal the couple's name and wedding date. Inside, they acknowledged their bridal party and parents, while also remembering family members who couldn't attend or who had passed away.  On the reverse side is a quote from the couple's favorite song.

**Reception paper:** Your bar area needs signage. Let guests know what signature drinks are being served and what is available at the bar so they don't have to guess (or ask!). The same goes for food or dessert stations. The simple detail of signage lets guests know what they're tasting.

## Décor

For this shoot, we wanted to give you a complete picture of designable areas for your wedding. Each detail was meticulously considered—even the food presentation. Pinpoint areas that matter most to you and have fun developing their personality. If you have a small budget, focus on areas that create the largest impact, such as your dining tables or food and beverage.

# Tablescape

**Centerpiece:** The biggest focal points of your wedding reception are the tables where your guests dine. We made a big statement with color and texture, represented in the pink and orange floral table runner that cascades to the floor. Think outside the box (and the vase!) and work with your floral designer to create something memorable.

**Place setting:** Since this shoot is all about pops of color, each place setting is anchored with a bright-orange glass charger. A gold stripe on the edge of the plates compliments the gold flatware.

Each place setting features a round, black-and-white menu card and a custom napkin in the signature pineapple pattern. If you can't find what you're looking for in rentals, consider having something custom made. The place cards are black with the guests' names written in white calligraphy, and a miniature gold pineapple. These little details add so much texture, style, and personality to the tablescape.

Consider substituting a champagne glass with a pre-set signature drink at each place setting, such as our champagne cocktail in miniature St. Germain bottles with a striped straw.

**Table and chairs:** A lucite table and chair lets color take center stage. The chairs have a striped back, as stripes were one of our design elements. Consider renting tables and chairs that feel more like furniture rather than the standard Chiavari chairs and round table with linen.

## Custom Lighting

The ceilings were high and our centerpiece was a flat floral runner, so we created drama and interest to connect the two. Custom bronze sequin drum chandeliers with crystals bring color to eye level and light to the tablescape. Put lighting on a dimmer switch so your planner can turn down the brightness when the evening calls for more intimate lighting.

## Escort Card Display

Our escort card display—the cards tell the guests where to sit—incorporated spray-painted miniature pineapples, shot glasses of glitter, and round escort cards. I love the color blocking and fun shapes in this display. We rented a white bookcase to display our escort cards, which became the ideal backdrop for this fun design element.

## Food & Beverage

Cocktails paired with food is a fun treat for your guests. The appetizers were inspired by a cocktail pairing rather than just the destination. Our caterer created three types of tasty combinations: quesadillas paired with lime margaritas in miniature tequila bottles, pulled pork sliders with a whiskey peach tea in miniature Makers Mark bottles, and a refreshing watermelon sashimi paired with a champagne and St. Germain cocktail.

We also created a beautiful dessert display with our favorite confections: pineapple sugar cookies, French macaroons, black-and-white cookies, and piña colada-flavored Jello shots. Give your guests dessert options besides wedding cake!

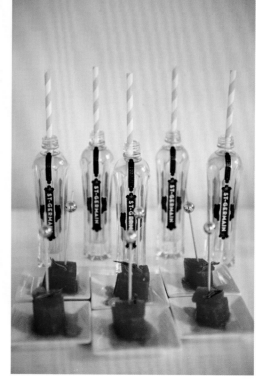

## Signature Drinks

The piña colada cocktail brings the pineapple theme full circle, with a pineapple wedge as garnish and a chevron-striped straw. Gorgeous glassware from Juliska enhances the presentation. Consider serving your signature drink in a fun glass, such as the gold pineapple cups on our bar cart.

Speaking of bar carts, why not display your signature drink in a separate location. Bar carts are fabulous conduits of design where you can set up trayed champagne and other spirits for your guests to enjoy at their leisure.

## The perfect piña colada

3 ounces light/white rum such as Mount Gay

2 ounces coconut cream

Pineapple and maraschino cherries to garnish

6 ounces fresh pineapple juice

2 cups ice

In a blender combine rum, fresh pineapple juice, coconut cream, and ice. Blend the first four ingredients until smooth. Pour into a hurricane or high ball glass and garnish with a slice of pineapple, maraschino cherries, and a striped straw.

## Gift Bags

The gift bags' bright pops of color are cohesive with our paper story, and, in keeping with the theme, contain items that are both practical and fun. Nichole Michel of Coral Pheasant Stationery + Design created the adorable pineapple tote, which is filled with pink and gold polka dot shot glasses, cocktail ingredients, and sweet/savory treats. The easiest way to dress up the welcome bag contents is to customize them. Our paper designer customized every detail down to the can of pineapple juice and the trail mix bags. This gift bag is inexpensive, yet packs a punch of personality!

## Photography

If you are planning a detail-filled wedding, be sure to give your photographers a list of the elements you want captured. Let the photographers know your wedding's color story and overall design scheme so they can think about what backdrops against which to shoot important details such as your jewelry, and how to incorporate your personal style into your portraits and family photographs. You have spent a lot of time executing these beautiful details, so make sure they are documented, especially since these details complete the story.

# MONTMARTRE
## Inspired by
### Watercolor Hues & Rosé

**M**ontmartre is an artist community nestled in the steep hillside above Paris, with sweeping views of the entire city. What better inspiration for our photo shoot than this creative community lined with narrow cobblestone streets, cafés, colorful veranda gardens, and talented street artists. At the heart of it all is the historic café La Maison Rose, whose soft pastel façade was a muse for Pablo Picasso, and our team.

Imagine a frothy blush pink gown, spring blooms in romantic watercolor hues, and hand-painted wedding invitations against this bustling backdrop of creativity and culture. We even found a talented silhouette street artist who created profiles of our bride and groom. Je t'aime Paris, indeed.

Alice Claire

Bruno Audrey

"*Paris* is always a good idea."
—Audrey Hepburn

# BEHIND THE DESIGN

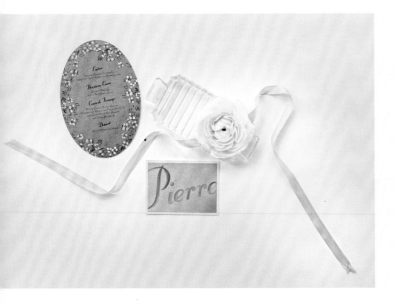

## Theme

When I think of Paris, I envision art, architecture, and romance, and those elements became the foundation for this shoot. When you dream of Paris, you may see something completely different. Perhaps the first thing that comes to mind is the rich food, the Eiffel Tower, or avant-garde fashion. Allow your own interpretation of a city or country to influence the look and feel of your destination wedding.

Here is how those three elements inspired us.

**Watercolor art:** We used watercolor art on invitations and stationery, a hand-painted wedding cake, wedding favors by a silhouette artist, and a tablescape that channels Georgia O'Keeffe. Since Montmarte has been an artistic haven for centuries, we embraced its history but gave it our own spin.

**Architecture:** No matter where you are in Paris, you are surrounded by something beautiful, and Montmartre is no exception. The famous, frothy pink cafe near Sacré-Cœur where Picasso and Dali used to hang (and sip rosé, I imagine) became our backdrop. In fact, we had been to this cafe on a previous trip, and the building's color inspired our palette. This is a wonderful example of how a location can become your muse!

**Soft colors:** In keeping with a romantic Parisian vibe, we chose soft shades of blush pink against a rich backdrop of red. The palette is muted, but color is used in interesting ways, such as the blush pink wedding gown. I love all the pink against pink in this shoot, and encourage you to play with a single tone-on-tone color in your weddings design.

## Fashion

The overall inspiration for this shoot was romantic watercolor hues and artistic details. It was important that the fashion reflect these elements.

**Gown:** This blush organza gown by Hayley Paige with three-dimensional flowers on the skirt was the perfect embodiment of our inspiration. It literally screams Paris in springtime!

**Accessories:** Even though your bridal shoe is rarely seen, it should reflect your gown's aesthetic. The rose gold peep-toe pump is the perfect complement to the bride's blush organza gown. Wandering the streets of Paris in heels can be daunting. It is always a good idea to have a backup shoe in the same heel height, such as a wedge or platform flip flop, that provides more comfort and support (especially if there are cobblestones involved).

**Beauty:** A soft blush palette for the makeup and a romantic up-do for the hair enhance the gown's feminine details.

## Paper

Every bespoke wedding has a story, and usually that story begins with paper. If you're looking to create something one-of-a-kind, consider hand painted invitations by an artist such as Kristy Rice of Momental Designs. Kristy kept with our style, using a soft, muted pearlesque paper which she then hand painted with flowers and the couple's names. An intricate lace ribbon ties the suite together.

This hand painted art found its way into all of our paper—from the flower illustrations on the menu cards to the curvaceous calligraphy on each place card. It also inspired the wedding cake.

# Tablescape

**Centerpiece:** Our colorful centerpiece was a mixture of antique crystal, found items, mirrored trays, and bell jars. We drew inspiration from the hand painted illustrations on the invitation and replicated them with real flowers. When I look at the table, I see a sea of watercolor hues perfectly balanced against our cream table. The arrangements are loose and organic, while the flowers are feminine and frothy (like the gorgeous Hayley Paige gown.). Let other areas of your wedding such as your attire influence and inspire your flowers.

The table is an example of how to introduce smaller arrangements and bud vases. Don't feel you need to do just one large centerpiece. Consider a grouping of fabulous arrangements in varying sizes and heights. The dimension and texture will make your dining tables pop and give each table a unique look.

**Place settings:** Hand painted place cards note where each guest is seated and show the time and care that you put into arranging your unique group of family and friends. A beautiful oval menu card sits on top of cream antique plates, accentuated by a single floral bloom.

We pre-poured a colorful blush signature drink at each place setting to give the glassware a pop of color. The wine glasses' stem shape is similar to that of the crystal cake stands and bell jars.

## Favors

We enlisted the talent of a local street artist to create unique silhouettes that guests could take home and have framed. Keep in mind your destination as you think of ideas for favors, and remember to gift items that can easily be packed into a suitcase and do not violate customs laws. Don't send your guests home with fruits, vegetables, or any type of plant.

## Cake & Confections

Erica O'Brien Cake Design re-created in edible ink the hand-painted flowers on the invitation. The organza flowers are the finishing touch. Inspired by the bride's gown, they symmetrically cascade down the cake's top and bottom layers. Simple in color and design, this cake looks almost too delicious to eat!

## Guest Gifts

Instead of having gifts waiting for guests when they arrive, consider sending a pre-wedding care package to get them excited.
We sent guests a travel note detailing important itinerary items, a box of French macaroons, a mini-bottle of champagne, and a coloring book of Paris. Other fun ideas could include a packing list, airplane travel kit, or food inspired by the destination. If this is too costly, consider sending it to just your immediate family and bridal party.

## Pets at the Party

As a doggy mom, I couldn't imagine celebrating my wedding day without my four-legged son, Winston, and if you're a pet parent, I'm sure you feel the same way! If you are having a domestic destination wedding, it is fairly easy to fly with your pet. If it's in another country, be sure to fully understand the laws regarding importing animals. When in doubt, it might be best to leave your animal at home.

## Photography

Take advantage of the local landscape for your portraits. Since architecture influenced the design, it was important to show unique architectural elements in the portraits and wedding party photos. Encourage your photographer to scout locations near your wedding venues. We found ourselves on the steps of the Eiffel Tower and along the cobblestone streets of Montmartre. Your surroundings and the provincial scenery should be their own "characters" in your photographs.

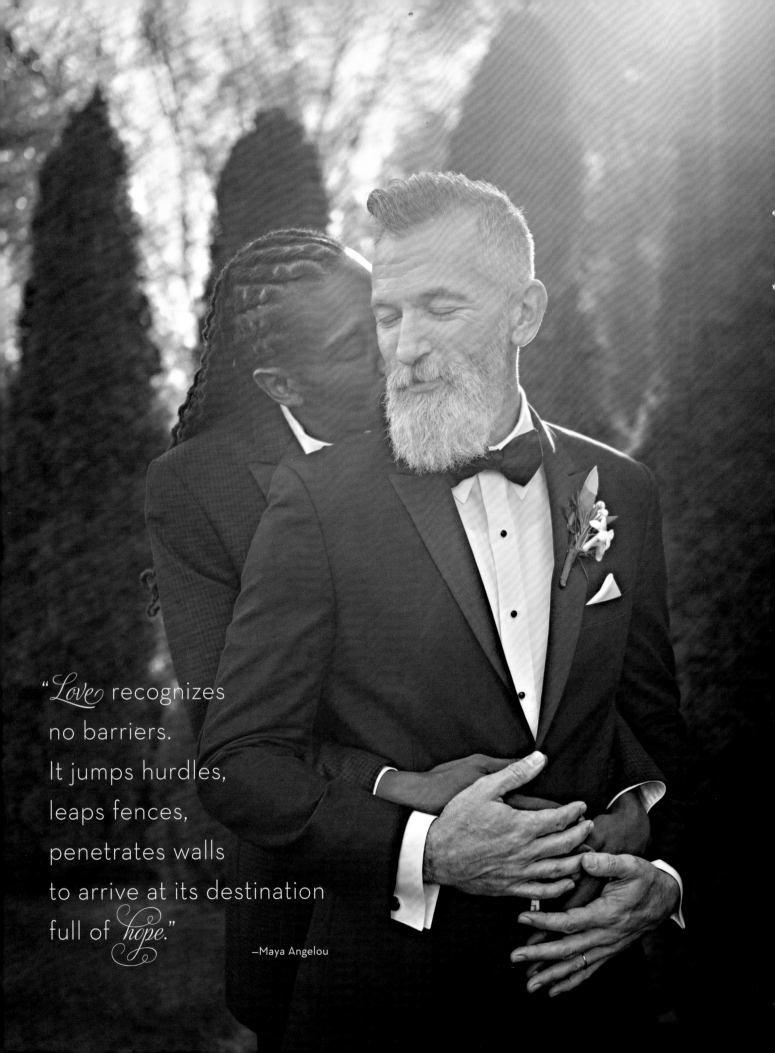

"*Love* recognizes
no barriers.
It jumps hurdles,
leaps fences,
penetrates walls
to arrive at its destination
full of *hope*."

—Maya Angelou

# NEWPORT
## Inspired by
### Boxwood, Leather & Chinoiserie

When you think of Newport, you may envision a stately mansion with boxwood hedges and classic décor. We do too, and that is why this shoot at Glen Manor embodied all of those elements, but with a modern flare. Take two handsome grooms, a traditional Newport mansion, add in a party of stunning bridesmaids in white dresses, a touch of leather and chinoiserie, and you have our vision of Newport, Rhode Island: a traditional celebration with a contemporary twist.

The thing we love about chinoiserie, our muse for this shoot, is that each pattern is unique, just like love stories.

www —
BRENDANCHARLES
— com —

www —
BRENDANCHARLES
— com —

— www —
BRENDANCHARLES
— com —

TWENTY SOUTH MAIN STREET | PROVIDENCE, RHODE ISLAND 02903

mr. and mrs. taylor sitzel
32 white chapel drive
mount laurel new jersey 08054

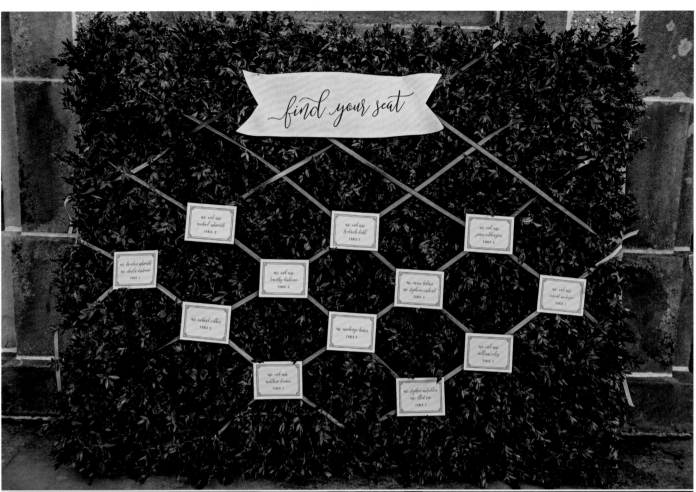

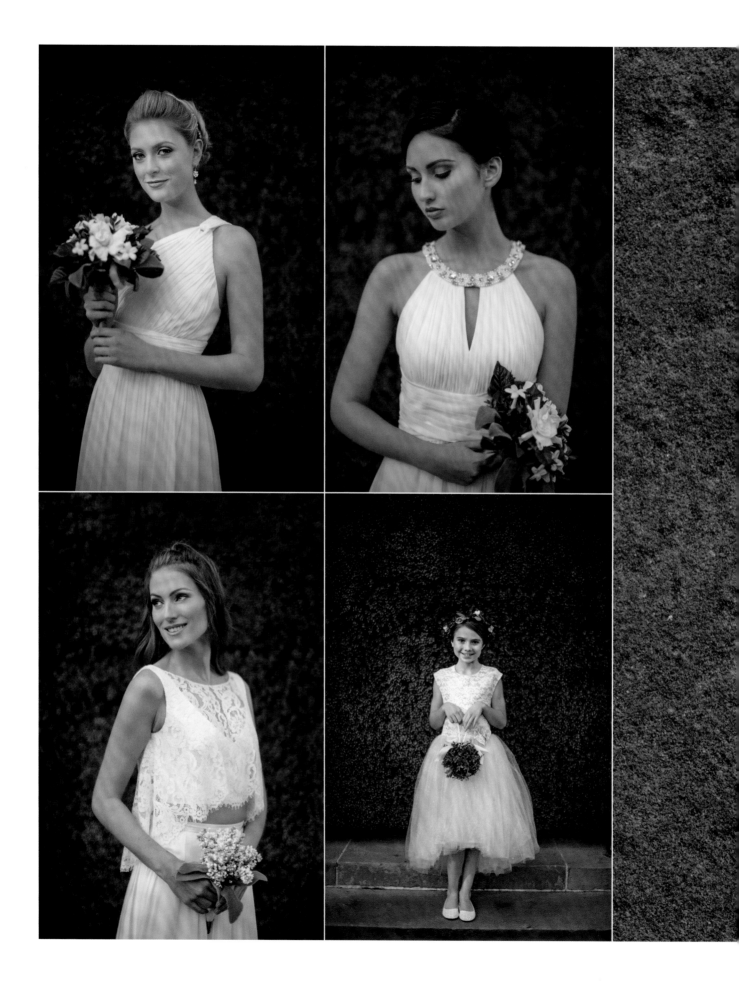

starlight royale
gin, lime juice and champagne

pear melba martini
vodka, chambord and pear nectar

sour cherry old fashioned
whisky, sour cherry
and orange zest

whiskey bar

LOVE MAKER
MAKER'S MARK BOURBON
GINGER ALE + LIME JUICE

JUST MARRIED JULEP
WOODFORD RESERVE WHISKEY
SIMPLE SYRUP + MINT

WHISKED AWAY
EVAN WILLIAMS WHISKEY
GRAPEFRUIT JUICE + BASIL

*starlight royale*
gin, lime juice and cha[...]

*pear melba* [...]
vodka, [...]

forever
and
always

THANK YOU FOR
CELEBRATING WITH US!

# BEHIND THE DESIGN

## Theme

Classic style with a contemporary, masculine twist is how we would describe the beautiful details that came together in Newport, Rhode Island. In an earlier chapter, I mentioned how family heirlooms can inspire details for your wedding, and that is partly what influenced this design. The classic blue and white European pattern, chinoiserie, sparked many details, from the color palette to the grooms' tuxedos. Family heirlooms provide more than just style—they ground your monumental occasion in your family histories as you join them together.

Here is how we incorporated our three key design elements:

**Pattern play:** Patterns can be intimidating, but don't be afraid to use them; they add a complexity and uniqueness. We folded this chinoiserie pattern into the table centerpieces, invitations, escort cards, and cocktail napkins—it even made an appearance on our bar chandelier. No matter what style of patterns you use, a good rule of thumb is to keep it simple and trust your instincts. If it looks too busy, it probably is. If it looks crazy but somehow works, go for it.

**Masculine textures:** In keeping with our two grooms' aesthetic, we wanted to ensure there was a consistent thread of masculinity throughout the wedding. We introduced textures like leather, greenery, marble, brass, and wood, combining them with softer accents. Natural materials such as wood and marble have become popular in weddings, and for good reason—they're easy to work with and play to a variety of styles. Soften them with fabrics and flowers, or embrace these hard elements by keeping your design clean.

**Traditional twists:** This couple embraced New England elegance but gave it their own spin. As you embark on planning your wedding make use of traditions you hold dear and part with ones that don't resonate. The personalized wedding is more than just monogrammed cocktail napkins— it offers the opportunity to incorporate whatever is meaningful to you.

# Fashion

This photo shoot was all about combining traditional and non-traditional elements with masculine and feminine details. Those themes were carried into the fashion by dressing the grooms in a twist on the traditional tuxedo and dressing the bridesmaids all in white!

**Grooms' attire:** We selected tuxedos for the grooms in the same color family, but one jacket is solid and the other is patterned so that each ensemble is unique but follows a common thread.

**Bridesmaids' attire:** Create interest in your bridal party by mixing and matching silhouettes and fabrics in the same hue. This allows each maid to choose her style and a shape that flatters her body type. While you are at it, give them each a bouquet of different blooms, but in the same color.

**White is the new color:** I adore an all-white bridal party. This clean color palette allows the wedding details to pop!

## Paper

The break with tradition started with our invitation. Nichole Michel of Coral Pheasant Stationery + Design composed a suite made of unusual materials, like the lucite invite. She went further and placed it in a box on a bed of boxwood. Remember when I mentioned that your invitation is the first glimpse your guests have of your wedding day? This invitation suite is a perfect example of how to tie the style of your day with your paper. From the leather tag and antique key to the quirky stamp placement, this paper story has all our elements wrapped into one.

If you have a bold idea for your invitation, enlist the help of an artist to take it to the next level. There are excellent resources online, such as the blog *Oh So Beautiful Paper*, for invitation designers who think outside the envelope.

## Décor

Comfortable, stylish lounge furniture became a focal point for this wedding. Creating unique seating areas apart from your dining tables gives guests the opportunity to gather, chat, and relax. They also make wonderful backdrops for photographs of family and bridal party, giving you the option of a *Vanity Fair*-style portrait.

The key to making the best use of lounge furniture is to place it in areas where people naturally congregate or where you want them to gather. During cocktail hour, place furniture near the bars. During dinner and dancing, create intimate lounges around the dance floor for those who want to rest their feet.

# Tablescape

**Centerpiece:** The focus is on beautiful chinoiserie bowls, vases, and containers. A whitewashed wooden table provides a neutral base, and our florist, Jane Brayshaw Rynaski, used a mixture of white flowers and greenery in keeping with the classic style. Finding chinoiserie vases proved difficult, so in some areas, we improvised with white porcelain vases. Mixing and matching containers gives each table a custom look. Add white pillar candles, and you have a romantic dinner setting.

To start collecting antique items for your wedding tables, visit websites such as eBay and Etsy and your local antique shop or thrift store. Check to see if your florist has something similar to save you the hassle. Replicas of the antiques used in this shoot have become popular **and** affordable. The truth is, your guests won't know the difference.

**Place settings:** We played up layers and metals. If your destination has unique rental options, consider sourcing fun flatware—like this bronze bumble bee pattern. A charger plate anchors each place setting, and while you may not be able to stack plates like we've done here, you can have a pre-set main course plate if you're hosting a wedding with a dinner buffet, action stations, or a family-style supper. If charger plates are not available, include a pre-set dinner plate that is removed once guests are seated.

**Chairs:** Decorating chairs is like putting the ribbon on a gift—it pulls the entire look together. We use boxwood greenery swags with a hint of navy ribbon to dress up the chairs at the head of the table. If budget allows, do something similar for your guest tables, or keep it cost-friendly and decorate just the bride and groom's chairs.

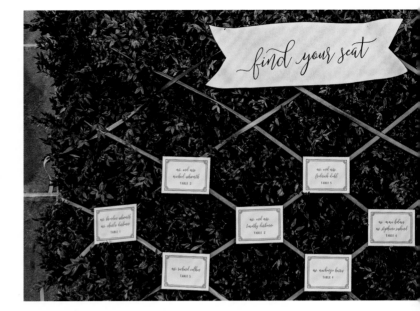

## Escort Cards

A boxwood wall displays the calligraphed escort cards that tell guests where to sit, and each contains a boxwood sprig. Arrange the escort cards in alphabetical order by last name so guests can easily find them.

## Family Heirlooms

Antique vases reinforce the family heirloom thread, but there are a lot of other ways to incorporate family tradition. Perhaps your grandmother has a handkerchief she used on her wedding day that you can borrow. Your father or grandfather could lend the groom an antique pocket watch that has been passed down for generations. If someone near and dear to you has passed away, consider affixing a piece of their jewelry to your bouquet or the groom's boutonnière.

## Food

The cozy fall weather inspired our menu and the culinary team at Blackstone Caterers. As you plan a menu with nods to your destination, incorporate seasonal dishes and ingredients, such as this starter course of pumpkin bisque. Keeping your menu seasonal and local will help to reduce expenses while giving your guests a regional experience.

## Signature Drink

We served classic gin and bourbon (even pairing them with desserts). Use simple glassware, or dress it up with unique glasses. If you can't afford to rent expensive glassware for your entire bar, consider serving only your signature drink in something unusual.

There is a lot of debate about the perfect martini, but we think this is the way a gin martini should be made!

## Gin martini with a twist

dry vermouth

2 ounces chilled gin

Pour a small amount of dry vermouth in a chilled martini glass and swirl to coat the inside of the glass. Dispose of any excess vermouth. In a shaker full of ice, gently swirl or stir the gin before straining into glass. Garnish with olives and a lemon twist (rub the rim of the glass with the twist).

## Cake & Confections

Our desserts were designed with all three inspirational elements in mind. The wedding cake has a bottom layer decorated to look like boxwood with the chinoiserie pattern on the middle layers. Our cupcakes have a monogrammed fondant topper painted to look like leather—complete with edge stitching!

The cake and desserts are styled on a wooden cart alongside our favorite amber spirits and paper chinoiserie napkins. Dessert displays don't need to be large and grand. You can also do something simple and elegant, featuring a smaller number of options.

## Guest Gifts

We decided on a comfort and travel theme, filling a monogrammed leather cosmetics case with tins of travel soap and included one of our favorite scented candles—pomegranate cider, a nod to the season. A trio of luxurious hand cream, artisan chocolate, and a leather luggage tag rounded out this gift. Our paper designer created a welcome note, luggage tag insert, and goodie tag. Wouldn't you love to find something like this waiting in your hotel room?

## Photography

A great way to combine your design elements and your portraits is to have your wedding party seated around the table before anyone eats. You have put so much thought into make sure every last detail is perfect, so why not have a photograph of you and your bridal party enjoying the beautiful tables? These types of photographs have become some of my favorites. I love the motion, conversation, and detail they convey.

# ARIZONA
## Inspired by
### Gold, Geometric Patterns, & Turquoise

What could be more romantic than eloping to the Scottsdale, Arizona, desert? We took design cues from dreamy golden sunsets, strong plant shapes, and pops of turquoise. The scheme came together in a sparkling gown against a desert backdrop; a random field of pink, wispy grass; deer antlers in the table centerpiece; and succulents in the bridal bouquet.

Michael Jane

Lewis Tate

# Menu

## HORS D'OEUVRES

CHILI-RUBBED CHICKEN & CORN TART
*with lime cream*

JAPANESE YELLOWTAIL
*summer melon and tomato*

CARAMELIZED ONION TART
*brie and red wine essence*

## ENTREÉS

PAN-SEARED HALIBUT
*white sweet potato purée*
*with truffle parmesan vinaigrette*

GINGER-BRAISED SHORT RIBS
*creamy polenta & roasted asparagus*
*korean ginger barbeque sauce*

## DESSERT

GOAT'S MILK FUDGE
*with candied lilac*

CHOCOLATE CUPCAKES
*vanilla buttercream icing*

"Oh that the *desert*
were my dwelling-place,
With one fair spirit
for my minister,
That I might all forget
the human race,
And hating no one,
love but *only her!*"
—Lord Byron

# BEHIND THE DESIGN

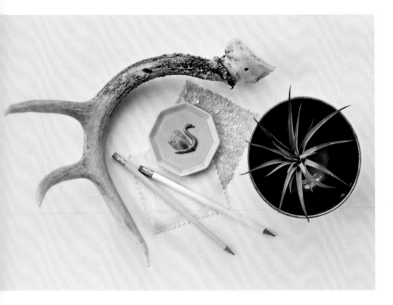

## Theme

Arizona's landscape is filled with inspiration, and we loved the idea of pairing soft, feminine design elements with the rough desert terrain. With a touch of boho and a lot of glamour, we set out to create an unexpected dinner party in an unexpected wedding destination.

These three elements pushed our ideas forward:

**Natural textures:** Air plants, succulents, sprigs of rosemary, and antlers were several of the natural textures we used. You can find them in everything from the bridal bouquet to the dessert display. As you think about your wedding's style, find ways to introduce the native landscape. Don't compete with your location's natural character. Embrace it and find ways to make it even more interesting.

**Metallics:** Gold! What's not to love? We are huge fans of this metallic color and always find ways to use it. We introduced this warm shade in the bridal gown.

There are no rules when it comes to metallics. Choose the metallic you like best, and if you want to be daring, consider mixing metallics. The key to using both silver and gold is to keep the rest of your color palette simple. Consider accentuating mixed metallics with one additional color, such as green.

**Unexpected sparkle:** We looked at the desert grains of sand and immediately thought of glitter. Our design theme contains a touch of sparkle, from the bridal accessories to the table linens.

## Fashion

I love the contrast between the Theia wedding gown's metallic jacquard fabric and the natural surroundings.

**Bride:** It is okay to have two very different looks on your day, but create consistency by sticking to one color palette. The ceremony look was classic and demure, so for the reception I styled her in a fully sequined sheath with dramatic gold accessories.

**Accessories:** Your veil should always be tonal to the color of your gown. To go with the gold gown, I selected a gold shimmer cage veil accented with an opulent brooch.

The silhouette and detail of your bridal shoe should always complement your gown. The strappy metallic heels are feminine with just a hint of edginess.

## Paper

Rustic-looking fonts, honeycomb-patterned letterpress, and unusual paper shapes stand out in this paper suite. Vanessa Kreckel of Two Paper Dolls is known for her innovative designs and swanky printing methods and techniques. Two aspects of a luxurious paper suite are paper type and printing method, and this letterpress suite looks refined.

Another standout detail is the dyed feathers that add a pop of color and texture. Ask your paper designer to come up with a similar idea using a natural element in your invitation design.

## Décor

The Monte Lucia property is landscaped with tall grasses and cactus gardens, so we embraced those features. Bridal accessories were shot against cactus leaves, and a field of pink grass was the backdrop for the couple's portraits.

## Tablescape

**Centerpiece:** Geometric shapes, such as the honeycomb pattern on the invitation, were repeated on the tablescape. Natalie Walsh of Hello Darling grouped together interesting containers and earthy antlers and air plants, adding a mix of textures with smooth porcelain vases, a rosemary garland, and sparkly sequin linen.

Ask your florist for a mock-up of the table design. This allows you to swap out items and curate your look.

**Place setting:** In contrast to the centerpiece, place settings are simple. We used a white dinner plate as a charger plate and wrapped rosemary stems with thin, bronze metal twine to give each seat added color and texture. Our paper designer created bracket-shaped menu cards in white and turquoise. The shape of our menus added an extra touch.

**Table runner:** Sequins can be a bold statement, and here the blush-colored, sparkly linen is softened with an "I Do" table runner from BHLDN. As you search for wedding décor, check out websites to add affordable and unique pieces. By mixing custom pieces with box store finds, you can elevate your look at a modest price.

## Flowers

Natalie from Hello Darling created this architectural lapel accent with braided leaves and a rich white flower. Boutonnières are the perfect detail to have fun with!

In the bridal bouquet, Natalie introduced gold metallic by spray-painting the leucospermums. Inside the bouquet you'll also find an antler, braided greenery, and soft blush flowers. It became an unusual and beautiful mixture of all our ideas!

## Cake & Confections

Angela Saban of Angel Cakes Bakery created a turquoise gem cake base entirely out of sugar and designed a honeycomb pattern in teal and gold. Your cake is a great place to combine several colors or design elements into one cohesive look.

The inside is just as important as the outside. Cake layers in our color palette are a sweet surprise underneath the blanket of fondant and buttercream.

On the dessert display, pistachio whoopie pies on a bed of sand (brown sugar) lend a desert vibe.

## Photography

Pay attention to the light! As you plan the wedding timeline, consult with your photographer about the best opportunities for portraits based on daylight. The timing of sunrise and sunset varies by destination, so consult a calendar such as SunriseSunset.com. Also, don't always call it quits when you think the light is gone. Many of our favorite images in this book were created just as the sun set. We would have missed them if we had stopped because there was no daylight.

# THE BERKSHIRES
## Inspired by
### Natural Winter Elements

The Berkshires, nestled in the western corner of Massachusetts, is the perfect destination for a winter wedding. What could be better than gathering your closest family and friends for a snowy weekend, with events centered around fireplaces, amber drinks, and hearty, seasonal comfort food?

Mr & Mrs Neeraj Najan
20 Ferrara Lake Way
Milford, Connecticut

I LOVE YOU BECAUSE I KNOW NO OTHER WAY
PABLO NERUDA

ADELINE & SAWYER
IVY GARDINER        JAMES HOLLOWAY

We humbly request the gift of your presence
as we are joined together in holy matrimony

December tenth, two thousand sixteen

Four o'clock in the afternoon

GEDNEY FARM
NEW MARLBOROUGH, MASSACHUSETTS

THE FAVOUR OF
YOUR REPLY IS REQUESTED BY
NOVEMBER ELEVENTH

M _____

accepts | rejects

384 GRANVILLE ROAD
WESTFIELD
MASSACHUSETTS 01805

Joseph Priestley
USA 20c

www.ADELINEANDSAWYER.com

ADELINE

HOLLOWAY

"Let us love *Winter*,
for it is the *Spring* of genius."

—Pietro Aretino

# BEHIND THE DESIGN

## Theme

The theme is winter glam, and Diana and Libby of Jubilee Events chose rich tones of navy blue, charcoal, burnt orange, and silver. Wood and fur were sources of inspiration—textures that reminded them of winter.

The following three design elements bring this vision to life.

**Crisp textures:** The winter season feels crisp—from the cold air to the twisted tree branches. Wood figures prominently in the design, starting with the setting in a rustic barn. Its walls provide a warm, enveloping backdrop to the party. The tall branches add height and texture on the table.

Metal offers another taut texture. Polished aluminum alloy dining chairs have a mirror effect, reflecting the wood floors, and metal candlesticks and a bronze charger plate add depth and sparkle. We mixed these materials with soft elements such as faux fur and feathers to balance the palette. A pony draped in garland even made an appearance!

**Rich tones:** Let the season inspire your color palette. Dark, rich tones are appropriate for winter, and they are perfectly balanced by all the winter white.

**Romantic lighting:** Candles on the table give off warm, amber light. The large marquee lights behind the tablescape provide an additional glow.

## Fashion

Winter glam means warm and cozy textures, smooth leather, and of course, sparkle!

**Bride:** Winter weddings are so much fun to style! In this photo shoot, the bride's fashion features layered textures created by a long-sleeve angora sweater dress, fox fur stole, and white leather gloves.

**Bride:** The angora gown was reserved for the ceremony and snow-filled outdoor photos. The bride's second look is a more traditional gown with a bead-encrusted bodice. The key is to wear a reception gown in which you are comfortable dancing the night away!

A dazzling statement necklace adds sparkle. When looking for a statement piece, check with family members to see if they have an heirloom that can be "something borrowed."

**Bridesmaid:** Layered textures make up the bridesmaid's attire, too. The lace bridesmaid dress offsets the simplicity of the bride's angora gown. It is accessorized with a vintage fur stole and velvet gloves. Don't be afraid to incorporate varying textures, especially for a winter wedding.

**Groom:** The groom is wearing a black velvet jacket accented by a navy velvet bow tie. Don't believe anyone who tells you that navy and black don't work together!

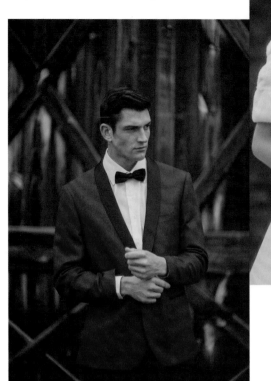

A groom can switch up his look by changing his jacket for the reception. The rich tone of this Marsala tweed jacket is in keeping with the wedding's color palette.

## Paper

Consider materials other than paper for the invitation. Nichole Michel of Coral Pheasant Stationery + Design crafted an invitation from wood. Laser-engraved wood is a unique medium for a rustic affair, and it has a lot of style with its natural color, texture, and scent. When I think of winter, I think of fur (faux and vintage only, of course). The invitation's envelope liner was inspired by fur and coincidentally, it is echoed in the reflection on the backs of our mirage dining chairs.

We also had fun with stamp placement. I love the centered vintage stamp on the RSVP envelope, which complements the color story. A special card was designed for the wedding website—and I encourage you to do a similar card if you develop an invitation with a suite of paper pieces.

## Décor

Decorations embrace the industrial barn setting and focus on seasonal snowy elements. The tall evergreen trees and nearby creek became a gorgeous backdrop for bridal portraits, while the wooded, snowy landscape inspired our color story.

## Tablescape

**Centerpiece:** The centerpiece has a tailored, masculine look. Yumiko Fletcher of Hana Floral Design used a variety of beautiful white blooms with a touch of burnt orange and a lot of greenery. I especially love the eucalyptus and evergreen. She lined the center of the table with crystal taper candleholders and mercury glass votives

We draped a fur blanket across the wooden table to add softness. Consider doing something similar with your winter-inspired tablescape. Another option is to drape fur along the backs of guests' chairs.

**Place setting:** Each place setting has a clear square charger plate with a fluted edge. We stacked a brown dinner plate and a clear bread and butter plate on top. A harp-shaped clip attaches the place cards to silver holders.

## Lighting

Since lighting was the third design element, we created a unique focal point. Ryan Designs, a lighting company, masterminded the spectacular LOVE sign and two bright X's and O's. Marquee lighting is popular and can be used in different ways. Consider putting a marquee sign behind your bar that spells "COCKTAILS" or "CHAMPAGNE." These lights also make great portrait backdrops.

When you walk into a room, the lighting instantly affects your mood. Warm, soft colors like candlelight create the intimacy captured in this shoot.

## Signage

Instead of using individual menus at each place setting, our paper designer came up with the idea to construct a large menu sign hung outside the barn. Signage is a great place to do something fun—you can create signs like this menu for virtually anything. Consider making large, bespoke signs in lieu of a ceremony program, for your bar menu, and any other area where you want to make a big impact. Having one large sign also eliminates the waste of individual pieces of paper.

## Cake & Confections

Consider serving several mini-cakes instead of one large cake. These are perfect for an intimate destination wedding and allow guests to experience many different flavors. The cakes are displayed on vintage silver candlestick holders, which brought in our metal texture.

Cute confections are displayed on a round, wooden table with a velvet and fur blanket. If you can't find the right linen, a blanket adds a lot of style (and can be used again in your home).

## Signature Cocktail

Our signature drink is the Whiskey Rose. We wanted something that reminded us of winter and included spirits that would keep our guests "warm." I encourage you to craft a signature drink around the season or location. If you're hosting a winter wedding, consider serving a spiked cider or mulled wine at cocktail hour.

## The Whiskey Rose

1½ ounces rye whiskey

½ ounce rosemary-infused simple syrup*

½ ounce lemon juice

sparkling apple soda

bitters

rosemary sprig and apple slice for garnish

Place a scoop of ice into a cocktail glass. In a cocktail shaker, stir together the whiskey, rosemary-infused simple syrup, and lemon juice. Pour mixture over ice and top with sparkling apple soda, then dash with bitters. Garnish each cocktail with a rosemary stem and apple slice.

*Bring equal parts water and sugar to boil with a sprig of rosemary; let cool.

## Photography

Animals give your images that little something extra. They can be unpredictable, so be prepared for some spontaneous fun! Make sure large animals, like our horse, Mr. Eddison, have their handler nearby to help set the stage and ensure the animal's safety.

# BARBADOS

*Inspired by*

*an English Plantation*

With its swaying palm trees, quietly lapping aquamarine waters, and a history rich with English traditions, Barbados is known as the gem of the Caribbean Sea. The island is proudly poised in the lesser Antilles, and among its rolling hills of sugar cane you can find the most exquisite plantations. We were inspired by the English architecture that peppers the island and designed a photo shoot with British flair.

Brightly colored tropical gardens, a hint of toile, playful flower girls, a long-sleeved gown inspired by Princess Catherine, and a sweeping view of the majestic East Coast of the island bring in all the wonderful nuances that Barbados has to offer.

Just because you are in the Caribbean, don't feel like you have to get married on the beach. Tropical destinations have much more to offer!

Together with their families

Rossana Graham
and
Jeffrey Curwin

Invite you to attend in
the occasion of their marriage
Three o'clock on Saturday afternoon
The twenty-first of January
Two thousand seventeen

St. Nicholas Abbey
St. Peter, Barbados

Sunset cocktails
and an evening of
dinner and dancing
to ensue

ST. NICHOLAS ABBEY

Mr. and Mrs. Richard Pearlman
5490 Middleport Crescent
Mississauga, Ontario L4Z3S5
Canada

THE
MARLON
HOTEL
NYC

US POSTAGE

Sunset cocktails
and an evening of
dinner and dancing
to ensue

— ❦ —

ST. NICHOLAS ABBEY

SUNSET C

Together with their families

Rossana Graham

and

Jeffrey Curwin

invite you to attend in
...sion of their marriage
...turday aft...

*"The sea,* once it casts its spell,
holds one in its net of *wonder* forever."

—Jacques Yves Cousteau

# BEHIND THE DESIGN

## Theme

When you think of Barbados, do you think of an English garden? We do! Barbados' history is rich with English culture (it's also known as Little Britain). We were inspired by our shoot location, historic St. Nicholas Abbey, and the architecture of the plantations that dot the island. The blue toile was the main design component in communicating an English garden look.

Here's how we pulled the look together.

**Bold pattern:** If you love patterns, consider picking just one and using it in a big way, as we did in blue and cream toile tablescape. A subtle watercolor pattern on the invitations in the same color story as our toile tie both patterns together.

**Tropical flowers & greenery:** Since we were in the tropics, it was important that any flora we used looked like it belonged. Everything—from the centerpiece to the bouquets—is native to Barbados. You don't always need flowers to achieve high style; greenery is extremely versatile, beautiful, and bountiful in the tropics. Don't be scared to go with an all-green palette, whether you're planning a modern or traditional affair.

**Vintage touches:** Barbados has a lot of history, and in keeping with our English garden look, we wanted to include elements with vintage elegance. We brought in vintage pieces, from bridal accessories to china.

## Fashion

The bride and her attendant were styled in looks that complement the romance and tradition of an English plantation. And, of course, a proper British wedding is never complete without a gaggle of precious little girls in frilly white dresses.

**Bride:** This long-sleeve lace sheath reflects the stately plantation aesthetic. It is appropriate to wear long sleeves in a tropical location, as long as the fabric is lightweight and the silhouette is manageable.

The reception dress has lace details and the same romantic sensibility as the ceremony gown. To maintain consistency between your ceremony and reception dresses, select gowns that are similar in fabric and style.

The lace veil completes the traditional English feel. When wearing a veil for an outdoor ceremony, consider one with lace, ribbon, or bead trim. These trim materials add weight that prevents the veil from blowing in the wind.

**Accessorize with local flora:** Select local plant materials to use in your boutonnière, bouquet, and accents, like the unusual seed pod boutonnière on the groom's lapel.

Our floral designer created beautiful flower-girl halos with beaded wire and attached colorful blooms.

This floral bracelet is a fabulous example of how you can make beautiful bridal-party jewelry out of flowers. It's also a great option for a mother-of-the-occasion who wants something unique that matches her outfit, as an alternative to the traditional corsage.

## Paper

The invitation suite, designed by Nichole Michel of Coral Pheasant Stationery + Design, marries our color story and love for toile. Since toile is such a strong pattern, Nichole used it for the envelope liner. The main invitation has a printed watercolor design with the verbiage in cream.

Instead of standard stamps from the post office, consider using vintage stamps that match the color palette. The blue stamps on our outer envelope add personality and color. Your invitation designer can source vintage stamps for you, but if you'd like to hunt for them yourself, check out Etsy.

## Décor

The natural surroundings inspired our décor. Take a look around and ask yourself—what does my location have to offer? What can I do to draw attention to areas that should be highlighted, and how can I enhance the space overall?

**Centerpiece:** We chose not to import or purchase anything for our tablescape, but rather, see what we could find growing around the island. With an abundance of greenery, we decided on a lush, foliage-only centerpiece.

Greenery has become popular in weddings, and the trend is here to stay. Ask your florist what greens are native to your wedding destination. If a leafy, viney look appeals to you, the Caribbean has plenty to work with.

**Place setting:** Layered china patterns are a main component of our table design. To achieve this look, find a charger plate that complements your table, like the rattan charger we used. Add a pre-set plate, like the gold loom pattern, and serve the first course on a patterned plate placed on top.

Rather than hiding the china with a napkin and menu card, we rolled the napkin with a leaf and used that to display a square menu. Have fun setting your table and don't be afraid to do something different.

**Linen:** Toile linen inspired our English garden tablescape, and we didn't want to hide it with chairs! The clear Louis Ghost Chairs have a traditional shape with a modern flare. Swapping out a traditional chair like the Chiavari or wooden folding chair with a more styled option adds character and polish.

## Escort Cards

Using the blue hues from our invitations, Nichole Michel of Coral Pheasant Stationery + Design created a clean layout on white cards. They were displayed on a series of wicker trays lined with tropical leaves.

Sometimes a design calls for simplicity, especially when an item must be functional. Displaying your escort cards on unique trays is a fun way to greet guests as they move from cocktail hour to dinner.

## Cake & Confections

Hope Butler, of A Little Imagination Cakes, was inspired by the watercolor on our invitation and the hibiscus in the bridal bouquet. The gorgeous flowers are made from sugar—and I highly recommend sugar flowers rather than real ones on your wedding cake. They can stand up to varying temperatures, don't have pollen or an odd taste, and look like the real deal.

## Signature Drink

Just like its name, Bajan rum punch packs a punch! A little sweet, a little sour, and definitely strong, it will only take a few of these to get the party started (you've been warned)! Serve it in a fresh coconut accented with a cute straw and the pop of a paper umbrella.

If you're getting married in the islands, consider having a coconut vendor at your wedding. They will cut open coconuts and serve up fresh coconut water to mix with your bar spirits (coconut water pairs best with a matured rum on ice). This is an entertaining and interactive way to level up the guest experience.

## Bajan Rum Punch

One of sour, two of sweet, three of strong, and four of weak
is the rhyme Bajans use to mix a rum punch!

1 cup freshly squeezed lime juice

2 cups Bajan raw cane sugar syrup

3 cups Bajan rum (look for Mount Gay Rum)

4 cups water

a few dashes of Angostura Bitters

grated nutmeg

slice of lemon or lime

In a pitcher, combine the wet ingredients well. Pour into glasses filled with ice, and add a dash of bitters to each glass. Grate fresh nutmeg over top and add a slice of lemon or lime. Cheers!

## Guest Gifts

We gifted a reusable jute tote (perfect for the beach), a striped towel, coconut water, flavored tea, a bottle of Bajan rum, Bajan sugar cakes, locally made chocolate, and a custom-designed cup.

If you're planning to visit your wedding destination before your wedding, don't forget to scout for these gifts. Live like a local for the day and see what fun items you can find that are authentic to the region. A wedding planner can also suggest items to include.

## Photography

Use your environment to create a narrative that incorporates the landscape. We ventured into a dense jungle on the property for photographs. I love how big the tree is compared to the bride!

# Planning Tools

## ACCOMMODATION DETAILS

|  | ACCOMMODATION NAME | CONTACT PERSON | CONTACT DETAILS | ROOM RATES(S) | # OF ROOMS RESERVED | #OF GUEST GIFTS TO DELIVER |
|---|---|---|---|---|---|---|
| Room Block #1 | | | | | | |
| Room Block #2 | | | | | | |
| Room Block #3 | | | | | | |
| Room Block #4 | | | | | | |
| Room Block #5 | | | | | | |

# VENDOR CONTACTS

| VENDOR TYPE | COMPANY NAME | CONTACT NAME | CONTACT DETAILS | CONTRACT AMOUNT | PAYMENT SCHEDULE |
|---|---|---|---|---|---|
| Band | | | | | |
| Bar Manager | | | | | |
| Bridal Dresser | | | | | |
| Bridal Salon | | | | | |
| Bridesmaid Dresses | | | | | |
| Cake & Confections | | | | | |
| Calligrapher | | | | | |
| Caterer | | | | | |
| Ceremony Musicians | | | | | |
| Ceremony Venue | | | | | |
| Cocktail Hour Musicians | | | | | |
| Décor | | | | | |
| DJ | | | | | |
| Entertainment (other) | | | | | |
| Florist | | | | | |
| Hair Stylist | | | | | |
| Invitation Designer | | | | | |
| Jeweler | | | | | |
| Menswear | | | | | |
| Officiant | | | | | |
| Photographer | | | | | |
| Reception Venue | | | | | |
| Rentals & Equipment | | | | | |
| Staffing | | | | | |
| Transportation | | | | | |
| Videographer | | | | | |
| Wedding Planner | | | | | |

# PLANNING CHECKLIST

## 12+ MONTHS

☐ Choose an ideal wedding date and discuss with those important to you.

☐ Write down what is important to you and compare your thoughts with those of your partner. What items are the same and where do you differ?

☐ Discuss your wedding budget and determine what you would like to spend.

☐ Confirm who will be contributing to your wedding budget.

☐ Compile a preliminary guest list.

☐ Research several destinations that are within budget and can facilitate your preliminary guest count.

☐ Research marriage and religious laws at your proposed destinations.

☐ Determine whether you will be legally married in your destination or in your hometown.

☐ Research wedding planners in your top destination or ones who are familiar with your destination.

☐ Discuss your ceremony preferences (i.e. church, beach, garden, etc.).

☐ Discuss your reception preferences (hotel, restaurant, historical property, etc.).

☐ Make travel arrangements to visit your top destination(s) of choice, if possible.

☐ Based on your research, select a destination that works best for you and your guests.

☐ Hire a wedding planner to guide you through the process.

☐ Begin research for a ceremony and reception venue.

## 9–12 MONTHS

☐ Draft your wedding budget, allocating funds based on what is important to you.

☐ Confirm your ceremony and reception venues with signed contracts and deposits.

☐ Research and purchase wedding-day insurance.

☐ Compile guest contact information, including mailing address and email addresses.

☐ Begin research and negotiations for hotel room blocks and vacation rentals close to your venue.

☐ Confirm accommodations for family, friends, and guests.

☐ Draft your wedding website, including important details such as date, time, location, and accommodations.

☐ Start your wedding registry.

☐ Review photography packages, options, and pricing.

☐ Determine if you want a photographer for the entire weekend or just on your wedding day.

☐ Review videography packages, options, and pricing.

☐ Determine if you want a videographer for the entire weekend or just on your wedding day.

☐ Book your photographer with a signed contract and deposit.

☐ Book your videographer with a signed contract and deposit.

☐ Compile a guest list for your engagement party.

☐ Set a location and date for your engagement party.

☐ Order invitations and thank-you notes for your engagement party.

☐ Mail your engagement party invitations.

☐ Begin to compile inspiration for your wedding day with the help of your wedding planner.

- [ ] Select your wedding colors and style.

- [ ] Complete your wedding registry prior to your engagement party.

- [ ] Choose your bridal party.

- [ ] Begin researching styles and stationery designers for your save-the-date cards.

- [ ] Order save-the-dates and include your wedding website. Mail your save-the-dates.

- [ ] Enjoy your engagement party.

- [ ] Make appointments at bridal salons to begin shopping for a wedding gown.

- [ ] Choose and order your wedding gown.

- [ ] Begin a preliminary timeline of your wedding day to stay organized.

- [ ] Send thank-you notes to those who attended your engagement party.

## 8–9 MONTHS

- [ ] Review options for an officiant based on marriage and religious laws in your destination.

- [ ] Select your officiant.

- [ ] Schedule an engagement photo session.

- [ ] Purchase outfits and accessories for your engagement session.

- [ ] Confirm engagement session location.

- [ ] Create a list of customs and traditions you would like to incorporate into the wedding ceremony and reception.

- [ ] Confirm when your gown is expected to arrive and schedule your first fitting (usually three to four months prior to your wedding date).

- [ ] Determine who will need wedding day beauty services.

- [ ] Research hair and makeup artists.

- [ ] Book your wedding day beauty team and schedule a trial, if possible.

- [ ] Compose your floral needs, including personal flowers, ceremony flowers, and reception flowers.

- [ ] Research florists in your destination and determine who might be the best fit.

- [ ] Schedule virtual meetings with florist candidates and your wedding planner to go over ideas.

- [ ] Receive floral quotes from more than one florist, if necessary, and select the right fit for you.

- [ ] Confirm your florist with a signed contract and deposit.

- [ ] Begin to plan your rehearsal dinner by researching options.

- [ ] Select your rehearsal dinner location along with the date and time.

- [ ] Begin to research invitation designers and determine if you want a custom or stock design.

- [ ] Receive quotes from invitation designers based on your preliminary ideas. You may want to include the rehearsal dinner invitation with your wedding invitation.

- [ ] Hire an invitation designer with a signed contract and deposit and begin the process of creating your invitations.

- [ ] Review your passports to be sure they don't expire within six months of your wedding date.

- [ ] Update your wedding budget to reflect current expenses.

## 7–8 MONTHS

- [ ] Begin to discuss your wedding day menu, including cocktail hour and the reception, along with what kind of service style you would like (buffet, grazing stations, sit down meal, etc.).

- [ ] Begin to discuss bar options with your caterer/bar manager.

- [ ] Receive menu options and make preliminary selections.

- [ ] Receive menu options for the bar and make selections.

- [ ] Schedule a tasting, if possible, with your caterer to make final menu selections.

- [ ] Discuss dessert options and determine if you want a wedding cake.
- [ ] Consult with your caterer and wedding planner on bakery options.
- [ ] Receive preliminary quotes for your wedding cake and desserts.
- [ ] Schedule a tasting, if possible, with your baker to make flavor selections and discuss style.
- [ ] Discuss your ceremony and reception entertainment preferences.
- [ ] Research songs for your ceremony, including the processional, interlude songs, and recessional.
- [ ] Hire musicians for your wedding ceremony and confirm with a signed contract and deposit.
- [ ] Compile a list of "must play" songs at your reception, including what you would like for your first dance, parent dances, and cake cutting.
- [ ] Determine if you want a band or DJ for your reception.
- [ ] Begin to research wedding reception entertainment.
- [ ] If hiring a band, ensure they can play the songs you've chosen for special moments.
- [ ] Hire wedding reception musicians and confirm with a signed contract and deposit.
- [ ] Book accommodations for your wedding week.
- [ ] Confirm where the two of you will get ready on the morning of your wedding.
- [ ] Discuss transportation needs for guests to and from wedding day activities.
- [ ] Discuss transportation needs for just your bridal party to and from wedding day activities.
- [ ] Receive and review quotes for transportation options.
- [ ] Book transportation after confirming flexibility should the number of guests, activities, location, and times change.

- [ ] If possible, make travel arrangements to visit your destination to hold meetings and consult with your wedding planner. Consider staying in one of the accommodation options you are offering guests to see what it's like.
- [ ] Schedule a table mock up, if possible, with your wedding planner and florist.
- [ ] Prepare images of hair and makeup styles you like for your beauty trial.
- [ ] Send hair and makeup inspiration to your beauty team. Be sure to include images of your attire and accessories.
- [ ] Choose invitation wording and send it to your invitation designer.
- [ ] Confirm your RSVP date for your invitations and how guests will RSVP (via snail mail or email).
- [ ] Review your guest list and make adjustments where necessary. Ensure all addresses are current and correct.
- [ ] Determine if you will hire a calligrapher to write your invitation envelopes, and if so, hire one with a signed contract and deposit.
- [ ] Send final guest list to your invitation designer or calligrapher.
- [ ] Finalize and order invitations.
- [ ] Schedule a meeting with your officiant.
- [ ] Schedule a time to visit your rehearsal dinner location.
- [ ] Update your wedding budget to reflect current expenses.

## 6–7 MONTHS

- [ ] Visit your wedding destination to make important in-person decisions.
- [ ] Do a walk-through of the reception venue with your wedding planner and caterer.
- [ ] Confirm what activities will be taking place and in what areas on the property.
- [ ] Schedule a menu tasting and make final selections.
- [ ] Confirm room layouts, table shape, and style of seating for the reception.

- ☐ Schedule a floral mock-up meeting with your florist and make adjustments as necessary.

- ☐ Enjoy your cake tasting with your baker and make your final flavor and style selections.

- ☐ Confirm your baker with a signed contract and deposit.

- ☐ Enjoy your beauty trial and make adjustments as necessary.

- ☐ Make appointments for bridesmaids to try on dresses.

- ☐ Make final bridesmaid and flower girl dress selection and have bridesmaids order their attire.

- ☐ Visit your rehearsal dinner location and finalize planning.

- ☐ Design place settings based on your food menu.

- ☐ Select linens, chairs, and all other rentals based on your site visit and aesthetic.

- ☐ Meet with your officiant and discuss ceremony items that are important to you.

- ☐ Confirm rehearsal and ceremony times with your officiant.

- ☐ Receive wedding invitations and prepare them for mailing by taking a complete invitation to the post office to have it weighed for postage.

- ☐ Based on your meetings, adjust your wedding day timeline.

- ☐ Update your wedding budget to reflect current expenses.

## 5–6 MONTHS

- ☐ Review your guest list and determine how you will track wedding RSVPs.

- ☐ Update your wedding website with current information, including transportation, if available.

- ☐ Mail your wedding invitations and get excited—this is happening!

- ☐ Begin to track your RSVPs and send weekly updates to your wedding planner on guest count.

- ☐ Confirm that all bridesmaids have ordered their dresses.

- ☐ Consult with your beauty team on a schedule for the day of your wedding and adjust your timeline as necessary.

- ☐ Book wedding day transportation for both of you to and from the ceremony, along with a getaway car after the reception, if necessary.

- ☐ Begin to research contents for your welcome bags, along with how you want to present these options (in a bag, box, etc.).

- ☐ If ordering custom tote bags or boxes, begin to design these.

- ☐ Order welcome bag totes or boxes and have them shipped to your destination. If that isn't feasible, determine how you will bring them.

- ☐ Begin to design your wedding day paper including programs, menu cards, escort cards, table numbers, and signage.

- ☐ Update your wedding budget to reflect current expenses.

## 4–5 MONTHS

- ☐ Begin to plan any activities surrounding the wedding, including excursions and a post-wedding brunch.

- ☐ Begin to write your vows, if desired.

- ☐ Purchase your wedding bands and if having them engraved, be sure to do so at the time of purchase.

- ☐ Research wedding attire for groom and groomsmen.

- ☐ Have male bridal party members measured for their clothing.

- ☐ Order male attire and choose accessories including tie or bow tie, cuff links, and shoes.

- ☐ Discuss your bridal shower with whomever is hosting it.

- ☐ Provide your bridal shower host with a guest list.

- ☐ Review your wedding registry and add or adjust items as necessary.

- ☐ Discuss the bachelor and bachelorette parties with your maid of honor and best man.

## 3–4 MONTHS

☐ Begin to take dance lessons, if desired.

☐ For the bride, purchase lingerie and undergarments for your wedding day attire.

☐ Choose bridal accessories, including your jewelry, shoes, and veil.

☐ Choose bridesmaid accessories, including shoes and jewelry. Purchase these items if they are a gift.

☐ Begin the alterations process on your wedding gown.

☐ Follow up with any outstanding RSVPs and adjust the guest count accordingly.

☐ If there are any last-minute invites, send those out now.

☐ Confirm with your wedding planner the total number of guests attending your wedding and any events surrounding your wedding. Be sure to include meal choices (if necessary), dietary restrictions, and how many children are attending, along with their ages.

☐ Update your wedding budget to reflect current expenses.

## 2–3 MONTHS

☐ Purchase gifts for your bridal party and parents to be presented at your rehearsal dinner.

☐ Purchase small items like your guest book, pen, toasting flutes, cake knife, and garter.

☐ Begin seating assignments for your wedding with the assistance of your family.

☐ Finalize seating assignments and send them to your wedding planner and caterer.

☐ Based on seating assignments, confirm the total number of reception arrangements needed with your florist.

☐ Based on final guest count, adjust and confirm your transportation needs.

☐ Choose ceremony ushers, greeters, and readers.

☐ Choose who will sign as a witness on your marriage license.

☐ Enjoy your wedding shower.

☐ Mail thank-you notes to those who attended or sent gifts to your shower.

☐ Discuss childcare needs with parents bringing their children and, if necessary, work with your wedding planner to offer them options for babysitters or nannies.

☐ Update the wedding website with any final information.

☐ Finalize all your wedding day paper and order.

☐ For the groom, if you would like a wedding day shave for you and your bridal party, ask your wedding planner or hotel concierge to help facilitate.

☐ If you would like a groom's cake, discuss with your baker and order.

☐ If purchasing wedding favors, determine what you would like to gift.

☐ Update your wedding day timeline.

☐ Review your upcoming final vendor payments and make provisions to transfer money or gather funds.

☐ Update your wedding budget to reflect current expenses.

## 1–2 MONTHS

☐ Begin shopping for attire for your wedding week.

☐ If leaving from your destination to go directly to your honeymoon, purchase clothing for your honeymoon.

☐ Confirm all final payments with your vendors and pay these in advance, if possible.

☐ Confirm all hotel and accommodation arrangements for yourself and guests.

☐ Have all final décor items you are shipping to your destination packaged and ready.

☐ Research and confirm shipping methods and timing to ensure your items arrive on time.

☐ If shipping to another country, ensure you understand the customs and duty laws.

- [ ] Ship any items that won't be traveling with you to your wedding planner, hotel, or venue.

- [ ] Confirm bridesmaids have their wedding dresses, shoes, and accessories.

- [ ] Discuss with your bridal salon the easiest and safest way to travel with your gown and make the arrangements they recommend.

- [ ] Schedule additional beauty appointments such as manicures, pedicures, spa treatments, and massages.

- [ ] Prepare a list for your photographer of family groupings and pairings you'd like to have photographed.

- [ ] Send the family shot list and timeline to your photographer for feedback and suggestions. Loop in your videographer if you've hired one.

- [ ] Finalize your family shot list.

- [ ] Determine who will emcee and give toasts at your rehearsal dinner and wedding reception.

- [ ] If you're planning to give a toast, begin writing it.

- [ ] Confirm all final quantities of flowers with your florist, including bouquets, boutonnières, mother/grandmother flowers, ceremony flowers, and reception flowers.

- [ ] Confirm delivery time and location of all personal flowers with your florist.

- [ ] Send song suggestions to your videographer for your wedding highlights video and full video, if desired.

- [ ] Send a final timeline and layout to your wedding caterer, including the number of guests at each table along with any dietary restrictions or allergies.

- [ ] Send final guest count to your baker and adjust the cake accordingly.

- [ ] Adjust your wedding day rentals based on your guest count and finalize.

- [ ] Order wedding favors.

- [ ] Confirm your final guest count and details with your wedding rehearsal dinner venue.

- [ ] Confirm your final guest count with any companies you've planned extra excursions or activities with.

- [ ] Confirm your final beauty count with your hair stylists and makeup artists. Also, confirm the original beauty timeline.

## 3 WEEKS

- [ ] If desired, send a pre-wedding gift in the mail to get guests excited about the trip.

- [ ] Create a packing list of all the items you will be bringing so nothing gets left behind.

- [ ] If you plan to change your last name, prepare all documents ahead of time.

- [ ] Confirm groom and groomsmen attire and, if renting, confirm delivery date and return date.

- [ ] For the bride, have your hair cut, colored, and styled, if necessary.

- [ ] Prepare a transportation schedule and confirm details with your transportation company.

- [ ] Make final adjustments to your wedding day timeline and distribute as necessary to your vendors.

- [ ] Confirm music choices with your ceremony musicians and give them a digital copy of your wedding program.

- [ ] Confirm music choices with your reception musicians including songs selected for special moments, such as your first dance.

- [ ] Send a digital copy of your wedding program to your officiant.

## 2 WEEKS

- [ ] Pack your bags and suitcases with all items you intend to bring to the wedding.

- [ ] Pack a separate bag and/or suitcase for your honeymoon.

- [ ] Withdraw cash for gratuity and any final balances due on arrival.

- [ ] If applicable, call your bank and credit card companies to let them know you where you will be traveling.

- [ ] Have your final dress fitting and pick up your wedding gown.

☐ Ensure that there is a steamer available at your destination to touch up your gown upon arrival.

☐ Make arrangements for cleaning and preservation of your gown after the wedding.

☐ Confirm travel arrangements by printing confirmations and having passports ready for travel.

☐ For the groom, pick up your attire and ensure it fits. Make adjustments as necessary.

☐ Ensure all groomsmen have picked up their wedding day attire.

☐ Email a wedding day itinerary to your bridal party and have extra copies printed to bring with you, just in case. Include the date, time, and location of the ceremony rehearsal.

☐ Email yourself important documents, such as your vows, wedding day toast, and ceremony readings in case they are forgotten or lost.

☐ Make copies of your passport to bring with you. Email yourself a digital copy, just in case.

☐ Cross-check your packing list to your suitcase and ensure all items are accounted for.

☐ Place cash in marked, sealed envelopes for final payments and gratuities. Keep a log of the amounts paid and to whom and ask for cash receipts.

☐ Have a final walk-through at your wedding reception location with your wedding planner and caterer.

☐ Assemble your wedding favors.

☐ Give your wedding planner all décor items, such as your wedding day paper, favors, and anything you brought with you for the wedding ceremony and reception.

☐ As guests begin to arrive, stop planning and start enjoying your wedding weekend. This special experience happens only once in a lifetime, so if anything is still left to do, ask a friend to help or forget it. Now is the time to have fun and enjoy all the hard work you've put into this special day!

## 1 WEEK

☐ For the groom, have your hair cut.

☐ Assemble suitcases and bags the night before you leave to ensure nothing gets left behind.

☐ Arrive to your wedding destination a few days before the festivities begin to manage last-minute tasks and logistics.

☐ Arrange to pick up your marriage license.

☐ Have a final meeting with your officiant, if desired.

☐ Put the final touches on your vows and give them to your officiant.

☐ Purchase items to go inside your welcome bags if gifting local fare.

☐ Assemble your welcome bags and delegate a friend or family member to drop them off where guests are staying.

# About the Authors

## CANDICE COPPOLA

Candice Coppola is the owner and creative director of Jubilee Events and Jubilee Events: Caribbean, an event design and planning studio with offices in Cheshire, Connecticut; and Barbados, West Indies. After launching her first company in 2007, she quickly became a sought-after event designer working with clients all over the world. Her signature feminine style is a mixture of the things she loves: bold colors, unexpected details, feminine touches, and anything and everything gold!

Candice fulfills her love for mentoring as the executive course instructor and tutor at the QC Event Planning School, working with aspiring event planners on a daily basis to achieve their career goals.

She has been a featured expert in *Brides Magazine*, *The New York Times*, CBS, NBC, *The Knot*, *My Wedding Magazine*, and *Modern Weddings Magazine*. Her work and voice can be seen in *Martha Stewart Weddings*, *ELLE Décor*, *Glamour Magazine*, *People*, *Elle Magazine*, *Inside Weddings*, *The EveryGirl*, *Style Me Pretty*, *Destination Weddings Magazine*, *Grace Ormonde Magazine*, *Bliss Celebrations Magazine*, and several other publications. She is an author of *The White Dress in Color* (Schiffer Publishing, 2011).

In 2014, Candice eloped with her husband, Jason, in a small church overlooking the Caribbean Sea. She now lives on the beautiful island of Barbados, planning destination weddings for clients around the globe.

### FOLLOW CANDICE

 @eventjubilee     @candice_coppola    @eventjubilee

# BETH LINDSAY CHAPMAN

Beth Lindsay Chapman is a stylist, bridal boutique owner, wedding fashion consultant, and veteran of the retail industry. Her love of bridal fashion, along with her sincere desire to create a memorable shopping experience for brides, compelled her to launch The White Dress by the Shore, a couture bridal boutique on the Connecticut shoreline, in 2004. She uses her expertise in fabrications, garment fit, and love of bridal couture to help clients select the perfect attire for their wedding. Beth is also the founder of Beth Chapman Styling + Consulting, a company that helps to uncover a bride's personal aesthetic and interpret it for their wedding day. In addition, she consults with bridal stores on elevating their brand through staff product knowledge and sales training. Beth's fashion artistry has led to styling editorial shoots around the world. Her work and voice can be seen in: *Wedding Bible*, *Simple Stunning Bride*, *Martha Stewart Weddings*, *Inside Weddings Magazine*, *Grace Ormonde*, *Brides Magazine*, *The Knot*, *WellWed Magazine*, *The Connecticut Bride*, *Bliss Celebrations*, *Gala Weddings*, *Southern New England Weddings Magazine*, *BrideLife Magazine*, *Style Me Pretty*, *100 Layer Cakes*, and *The White Dress in Color*, her first book. Beth resides in Guilford, Connecticut, with her husband, Mark, their two children, and their fur baby, Mr. Pickles.

FOLLOW BETH

 @bethchapmanstyling       @beth_styling       @bchapmanstyling

# CARLA TEN EYCK

Carla has been joyfully photographing weddings for the past fifteen years all over New England and beyond. She received her BFA in photojournalism from the Rochester Institute of Technology in 1995. Her photojournalism field work includes working at *The Hartford Courant*, *The Rochester Democrat and Chronicle / Times Union*, and The Associated Press in New York City. Carla's segue into documenting weddings was natural and combined her best skill sets of photographing people, moments, and emotions with style, beauty, and a sense of humor. Carla also has amazing crowd control skills. Maybe being one of nine children helped with that!

Carla runs a boutique studio out of her renovated childhood home in Hartford, Connecticut's historic West End, where she is also raising her amazing children, Jackson + Georgianne.

Carla is an author of the inspirational coffee table book *The White Dress in Color*. She is also the photo director for Engage Luxury Business Summits, a former coproducer of Inspire Photo Retreats, and has given motivational speeches to wedding professionals throughout the US.

Carla's second love is teaching and mentoring. For more than twelve years, she has been teaching workshops all over the world and mentoring businesses to reach the next level.

Always the storyteller, Carla started a podcast, "Eyes Up Heart Open," in 2016 to share how we are, ultimately, all connected. There she shares openly about her life, family, and struggles, and interviews people in her life who have amazing stories to share.

Carla works hard to enthusiastically breathe energy, excitement, and fun into everything she does, from turning ideas into reality, to shooting in new locations around the globe, and to simple things like snuggling with her kids Jack + GG, their kitties Mr. Moo + Trix Mix, and hiding in the studio trying to scare everyone!

## FOLLOW CARLA

 @c10ike      @carlateneyck     @carlateneyck

# Credits

## PALM BEACH

**CAKE:** Ana Parzych Cakes

**CATERING & BLACK/WHITE COOKIES:** Emily's Catering Group

**CUSTOM BAR & CHANDELIERS:** Ryan Designs

**FLORAL DESIGN:** Diane Gaudett Custom Floral Designs

**FURNITURE RENTALS:** Luxe Event Rentals

**GLASSWARE:** Juliska

**GOWN:** Hayley Paige

**HAIR:** Catie & Amy

**JEWELRY:** Aquinnah

**LINENS:** La Tavola Fine Linen

**LOCATION:** The Loading Dock, Stamford, CT

**MACAROONS:** Le Petite France

**MAKEUP:** Jennie Fresa of Jennie Fresa Beauty

**MODELS:** Bride: Chelsea Bennett Colonese; Groom: Michael Daley Caserta; Bridesmaid: Maggie, Inc.

**PAPER, CUSTOM NAPKINS & WELCOME BAG:** Coral Pheasant

**PINEAPPLE COOKIES:** Sweet Marias

**SHOES:** Kate Spade

**STRIPED DRESS & RECEPTION DRESS:** Kirribilla

**SUIT:** J. Crew

**TABLEWARE RENTALS:** Party Rental Ltd.

**VINTAGE PROPS & PROP STYLING:** House of Michel

## MONTMARTRE

**BELT & EARRINGS:** Maria Elena Headpieces & Accessories

**CAKE:** Erica O'Brien Cake Design

**FLORAL DESIGN:** Just For You Floral Design LLC

**FURNITURE RENTALS:** Jubilee Events

**GOWN:** Hayley Paige

**HAIR:** Yoshiko Haruki

**LOCATION OF TABLESCAPE:** Wadsworth Mansion

**MACAROONS:** Biscuiterie de Montmartre

**MAKEUP:** Yoshiko Haruki

**MENSWEAR:** Valentino Tailors

**MODELS:** Bride: Liane Boyko; Groom: Alex Winter

**PAPER:** Hand Painted Stationery—Momental Designs

**RING & BRACELET:** Haute Bride

**SHOES:** Badgley Mischka

**TABLEWARE RENTALS:** Jubilee Events

**WELCOME GIFT:** Jubilee Events

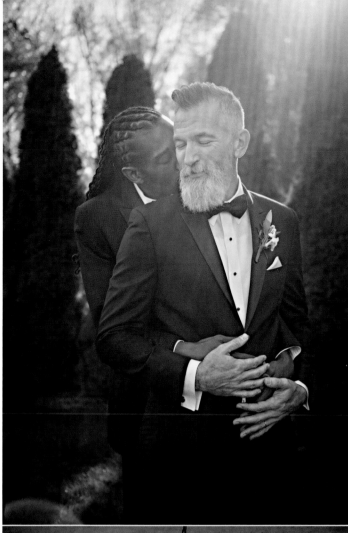

# NEWPORT

**BODY JEWELRY:** Sara Gabriel

**BRIDESMAID DRESS:** Theia & Donna Morgan

**CAKE & CUPCAKES:** Something Different Cake Couture

**CATERING:** Blackstone Caterers

**CHANDELIER:** Ryan Designs

**EARRINGS:** Haute Bride

**FLORAL DESIGN:** Just For You Floral Design LLC

**FLOWER GIRL DRESSES:** Chasing Fireflies

**FURNITURE AND SET PIECES:** Party by Design Greater Boston Area

**HAIR:** Adriana Bomova of The Beauty Bar

**LEATHER TRAVEL CASE:** Felix Street

**LOCATION:** Glen Manor House

**MAKEUP:** Simply Gorgeous by Erin Infantino

**MODELS:** Grooms: David Hand & Anthony Watson; Bridesmaids: Maggie, Inc.; Junior Bridesmaid: GeorgieTen Eyck; Flower Girl: Caroline Ferdenzl

**OUT OF TOWN BAG:** Jubilee Events

**PAPER:** Coral Pheasant

**PAPER NAPKINS:** BHLDN

**SCENTED CANDLE:** Simple Lights Candles

**TABLEWARE RENTALS & BAR CART:** Be Our Guest, Inc.

**TUXEDOS:** Aldo's House of Formals

**VINTAGE PROPS & PROP STYLING:** Nichole Michel, House of Michel

## ARIZONA

**ACCESSORIES:** Maria Elena Headpieces & Accessories

**CAKE & CONFECTIONS:** Angela Saban of
      Angel Cakes Bakery

**FLORAL DESIGN:** Hello Darling

**GOWN & RECEPTION DRESS:** Theia

**HAIR & MAKEUP:** Tara Dowburd owner of Makeup Therapy

**LINENS:** La Tavola Fine Linen

**LOCATION:** Montelucia Resort, Scottsdale, Arizona

**MODELS:** Bride: Pauline Van Valin; Groom: Jamal Lewis

**PAPER:** Two Paperdolls

**SHOES:** Nina

**TABLEWARE RENTALS:** Classic Party Rentals

**TABLE RUNNER:** BHLDN

**TUXEDO:** Mr. Formal of Arizona

With special thanks to Victoria York

## THE BERKSHIRES

**BRIDESMAID DRESS:** Amsale

**CAKES:** Elisabeth Palatiello - But A Dream Custom Cakes, LLC

**DESIGN:** Diana Chouinard & Elizabeth Basile of Jubilee Events

**EARRINGS & NECKLACE:** Haute Bride

**FLORAL DESIGN:** Yumiko Fletcher of Hana Floral Design

**FUR:** Provided by Stylist

**FURNITURE AND SET PIECES:** Modern Reserve Rentals

**GLOVES:** Carolina Amato

**GOWN & BELT:** Ivy + Aster

**HAIR:** Emily Reale

**LIGHTING:** Ryan Designs

**LOCATION:** Gedney Farm

**MAKEUP:** Erica T. Martell

**MENSWEAR:** Valentino Tailors

**MODELING AGENCY:** Maggie Inc.

**PAPER:** Coral Pheasant

**PROP STYLING:** Nichole Michel, House of Michel

**RECEPTION DRESS:** Kate McDonald Bridal

**TABLEWARE RENTALS:** Rentals Unlimited

# BARBADOS

**BRIDESMAID DRESS:** Amsale

**BRIDESMAID JEWELRY:** Haute Bride

**CAKE:** A Little Imagination Cakes, LLC

**CHAIRS & TABLE:** Milestone Events Barbados

**FLORAL DESIGN:** Tony Palmieri for Green Dahlia

**FLOWER GIRL BASKET & TOSS PETAL BAGS:**
Pressed Cotton

**FLOWER GIRL DRESSES:** Ivy + Aster

**GOWN & VEIL:** Amy Kuschel

**HAIR:** Maria O'Neal

**HEADPIECE:** Maria Elena Headpieces & Accessories

**JUTE BEACH BAG:** From Sir with Love

**LOCATION:** St. Nicholas Abbey

**MAKEUP:** Leah Whitehead

**MODELS:** Bride: Lee Tryhane; Groom: Sacha Soodeen;
Bridesmaid: Ina Bishop

**OUT OF TOWN BAG:** Jubilee Events

**PAPER & CUSTOM MUGS:** Coral Pheasant

**SHOES:** Badgley Mischka

**SUIT:** Provided by Model

**TABLEWARE RENTALS & LINEN:** Party Rental Ltd.

**TIDBIT PLATES:** BHLDN

**VINTAGE PROPS & PROP STYLING:** Nichole Michel,
House of Michel